The 10-Day Total Body Transformation

A DOCTOR'S GUIDE TO GETTING LEANER, CLEANER, AND HAPPIER IN JUST 10 DAYS!

SHILPI AGARWAL, M.D.

For my dad,
my inspiration, my angel. I love you!

For my husband,
my best friend, my rock. I adore you!

Internet addresses given in this book were accurate at the time it went to press.

Printed in the United States of America

Interior design by Joanna Williams
Cover photo by Jof Panlaqui

Library of Congress Control Number available upon request

ISBN 978-0-9994151-6-0

2 4 6 8 10 9 7 5 3 1 paperback

Visit our parent company at MomosaPublishing.com

Contents

Introduction

Hi, I'm Dr. Shilpi. Nice to meet you! A lot of people ask me for health advice. Maybe it's because I have the letters "M.D." after my name or because you have seen me on TV talking about everything from smoothies to Spanx. It may also be because you know me as a shameless health trend addict, willing to test-drive any and all new diets, workouts, and wellness fads.

As a physician, woman, and mom, I hear, see, and live through the struggle of staying healthy every single day. That's why I'm always on the lookout for the latest, greatest shortcuts, innovations, and health habits that will make my life (and the lives of my friends and patients) much easier.

I can honestly say this whole health and wellness frontier isn't just my area of expertise; it's my biggest passion. It's kind of always been my thing, and for as long as I can remember, I've been devoted to testing the newest, hottest, and craziest health trends. You probably can't name a cleanse, class, or fitness routine I haven't tried.

Maybe you've seen me sweating from my eyebrows to my undies in Bikram yoga (even Nelly would find it hot in there) or explaining to my husband that the $200 charge on our credit card statement for a "juice cleanse" was a legitimately important personal and professional investment (love you, honey!).* You name it, I've tried it.

So after all my years of professional experience and personal experimentation (not to mention thousands of hours treating patients), what have I learned? A lot. But there's one specific area I see women of all ages getting hung up on. Ladies, the scale alone does not paint the full picture of your overall health. True health is about so much more than just your weight. I hate to give it all away up front, but living your best life (yep, I just Oprah-ed you) and achieving real, sustainable, effortless health and wellness are a matter of majorly making over your food and lifestyle habits and getting your mind on the path to wellness.

*For the record, I did cheat during that juice cleanse. While, I'm not proud of that, the cheese stick I ate was absolutely worth the shame, *and I have no regrets. My husband, on the other hand, did not cheat (of course), and he says he successfully reached that supposed post-juicing euphoria, while I successfully turned over every kitchen cabinet in search of solid food.*

Research has shown us time and time again that dieting doesn't even work, and chasing the skinny ideal at any cost is not a surefire solution to all your problems. Diets don't work. I'm gonna go ahead and repeat that and hashtag it, because it's that important: #DietsDontWork. Bam. We know this from research and real life.

I'm guessing you're here because you've accumulated a bunch of diet books, or you've bookmarked a ton of healthy blogs, and you've dropped some dough on celebrity-endorsed waist cinchers and skinny pills. If you want to start shedding extra weight immediately, I suggest throwing all those things into the trash, along with your Ab Roller, and take a moment to get centered and think about what true health would really look like if you got serious about self-care. (Hint: It might not mean a six-pack or thigh gap. It might mean climbing the stairs without getting winded.)

Look, pretty much everyone has fat pants. I know that I do. You probably do too. Maybe you break them out every holiday season to accommodate for some pumpkin spice–induced weight gain. Or maybe they're more of a consistent wardrobe staple, and you feel like you're wearing them more often than you'd like. Whatever the case, my hope is that when you're done with this plan, you'll ditch your fat pants and have the tools to make better choices so you can see, feel, and experience a real, lasting difference in your physical and mental health.

• • •

As a child, I remember hearing my dad repeat two go-to mantras: "Health is wealth" and "Prevention is better than cure." But it wasn't until I was older that I realized how much value these statements really hold. Although I was fortunate to grow up in a home where I had a healthy and home-cooked dinner every night and a packed lunch for school every day, I wasn't exactly healthy—not by a long shot. My diet was filled with processed snacks that contributed to being overweight. I tried to shrug off the extra cushioning as baby fat, but I don't think you can convincingly call it that when you're so far past the baby stage that you can legally drive a car. There's nothing inherently wrong with being bigger, but in my case, and maybe in yours, my extra pounds were definitely indicative of bigger issues.

I grew up during the era when "fat-free" was king, and even saying the word "fat" was considered worse than saying the other F word. (It's the one that autocorrects to "duck" in my phone. Every. Ducking. Time.) Many of the foods I was eating contained refined sugars, artificial sweeteners, and lots of other additives that scientists are only now discovering to be super toxic. Scary, right? I was filling my body with junk, and it showed, both in how I looked and how I felt.

After medical school, I was fortunate to move to Los Angeles for my residency training. What you've seen on screen and in US Weekly is true: LA is the international capital of health and wellness and home to the hottest health trends, partly thanks to Hollywood. After living in LA for some time and meeting the top trainers, health food experts, and physicians in my field, I truly realized the fact that "healthy" isn't a look; **it's a way of life.** It's not a diet or a workout routine but a day-to-day commitment. Becoming lean and clean means adjusting how you look at food and the choices you make, and examining both your physical and mental goals.

The point of The 10-Day Total Body Transformation isn't to encourage restriction or obsession over food. That will leave you feeling deprived and frustrated, and it will also set you up for failure. Not to mention, significant restriction can also create unhealthy patterns that lead to long-term health consequences. The true intent of this program is to equip you with the tools you need to finally take control of your mind and body and transform your life. Are you with me?

Why This Plan Is Different from the Other 5,678,972 You've Tried

You'll never hear me say it's time to give up all carbs or commit to eating two cucumbers with lemon and cayenne pepper for breakfast, lunch, and dinner. (Sorry, Bey, I love you, but I'm sad you did that Master Cleanse back in the day.) This book won't feed you more crazy claims and unrealistic expectations. Instead, it will address the nutritional, physical, and mental aspects of being healthy and help you actually make sense of the confusing, contradictory health stories you read about all the time.

Every day, I teach patients how to work at being healthy. I'm not exempt from this constant commitment: I have to practice what I preach. During The 10-Day Total Body Transformation, I'll show you exactly how you can use a few simple principles to get leaner, cleaner, and happier. Will you lose weight if you follow this program? Yes! (Woo hoo!) But this book is about so much more than fitting into a smaller dress size or a sexy new pair of skinny jeans. (But by all means, go shopping and treat yo'self on day 10.) The 10-Day Total Body Transformation is all about improving the way you think and feel—about yourself and the world around you. By the time you complete this program, you'll know what it's like to feel better, fitter, stronger, and happier, and you'll finally have what it takes to tackle your physical and mental goals.

The truth is, this is going to take work and commitment. But if you're willing to go on this journey with me, then get ready to completely transform your body and your mind in the next 10 days. How will you do that? By mastering the lessons I'll teach you so that you're equipped with the tools to continue staying healthy for the rest of your life. I promise!

I'm going to teach you how to take charge of your diet and life and become the healthiest you've ever been. You'll also learn and use some of the most common celebrity health tricks to get lean and clean. Making a change in your diet and lifestyle is a big step, but you will feel the benefits. And because this is a lifelong journey and we all have setbacks and slipups, you can always rely on these tools to steer you back onto the right path so you can continue to become the best version of yourself.

Okay, Dr. Shilpi, Sounds Great! But How Do I Know This Is the Program for Me?

- If you need more energy, this book is for you.
- If you're in a "fat" phase, this book is for you.
- If you're spending most of your nights bringing the #party home from the pub, this book is for you.
- And hey, guess what? If you've tried everything (raising my hand), this book is for you.

The fact is, more than 43 percent of women admit to being more stressed today than they were five years ago.[1] Take a moment and think about whether you fall into that frazzled group. This constant stress has a direct impact on your health and happiness. It can cause you to binge on high-sugar foods, and it can bring about headaches, weight gain, poor sleep, and bad skin while contributing to long-term problems such as chronic fatigue and high blood pressure. What's more, 50 percent of Americans say they don't have enough energy, and 29 percent are seriously dragging their tails several times a week, according to the American Psychological Association. Are you one of the statistics?

This book will also help you become more aware of who you are. When you truly commit to the idea that you control your thoughts, behaviors, experiences, and relationships, you can begin to enjoy your life and feel happier every step of the way. In just 10 days, you will understand the fundamentals of controlling your outlook and ultimately your mind and body.

So How Is This Going to Work Exactly?

I would love to tell you to head straight to Miraval Resort for a relaxing 10-day reboot complete with catered meals and round-the-clock spa services, but the reality is…well, that's just not reality. For any new health habit to be effective, it's important for it to be easy to follow and simple enough that you can incorporate it into your daily life. All too often, I see patients, friends, and family go on diets and lose weight, gain weight, and then start back at square one. This happens because these diets are not sustainable ways of life, or they're so complicated no one can keep up. You need to calculate calories, subtract carbs, and add three points for protein? I'm already lost! Instead, I will give you guidelines that are simple and easy to follow.

Nowadays, we have more going on in our lives than ever before. We check our email while we pee, we drink our coffee while signing our kids up for summer camp, and we grocery shop while waiting for an Uber. This is the nature of life today. Adding in a rigorous and detailed food schedule is the last thing anyone wants or needs. Instead, I'm here to help you become the best version of yourself by focusing on healthy habits that are easy to incorporate into your life.

Getting to Homeostasis (and What the Heck That Means)

Big word, simple meaning: Homeostasis is your body's ability to maintain internal stability. Even though it may feel like your waistline (or butt or thighs or...) is out to sabotage you, your body is very sophisticated. It always resists change to maintain balance. Homeostasis is this concept of balance.

When given the choice, your body will always stay at the same weight and same general state of health—unless a significant outside force interferes. If you are normally pretty healthy and maintain a stable weight, indulging in a cheeseburger and fries probably won't cause you to pile on real pounds or body fat because your body is wired to regain equilibrium. Sure, you might feel full and bloated, but those things are temporary; feelings aren't facts. But on the flip side, one salad and a jog around the block won't produce much change if your lifestyle includes frequent fast food and an unused gym membership. Sorry!

Change in either direction happens over time. This is due to your body's primitive instinct to maintain itself where it currently exists. Your body regulates itself to maintain a specific degree of body weight homeostasis, and it understands how to operate within this set of norms. If you're really trying to shift your body's norm, you're going to have to make a significant change. With the 10-Day Total Body Transformation, you'll make that kind of change. Over time, implementing these tips and tricks will become effortless and even enjoyable. I promise!

But "significant change" doesn't have to equal punishing, all-or-nothing rules around food and fitness. It means knowing where to focus your efforts. I subscribe to the 70/30 rule: To achieve and maintain a healthy body and weight, 70 percent of your efforts should focus on dietary changes, and 30 percent should focus on exercise. You can't reach your 100 percent personal best without both. Not a day goes by at the office when I don't hear a patient tell me they eat well but don't exercise, or I meet a woman at the gym who exercises for two hours a day but then tears open a big bag of chips for dinner. Exercise and healthy eating go hand in hand. Modifying your diet *and* exercise routine is the only recipe for a life of lean and clean success. But you're not in this alone. I'm here to help you understand how to do this in a way that's simple, smart, and actually sustainable.

You will be learning a lot of information in the next chapters. But don't worry! I've got your back!

Look for the summaries and takeaways at the end of each chapter.

So now that you know the game plan, are you in? Let's go!

Summary

In order to help you on this journey, I have provided a summary at the end of each chapter. Look out for this page to get the most important themes and points from each section.

You can use the section summaries to take notes and jot down your questions and goals.

If you have questions, share them with the 10-Day Total Body Transformation community on social media. Use #10DayTBT to find others and join the community.

1

Nutrition and Diet

Getting into the zone of healthy means understanding the role of nutrition and diet in your life. There is a lot of information out there, but some is conflicting and most is simply too confusing to understand, much less use in real life. Here is a breakdown of all the nutrition basics without the fuss or Ph.D. studying required. Pay close attention because once you grasp these concepts, you can use them to make smarter and more informed choices for the rest of your life. Additionally, you can use this knowledge to decode foods and find out what's really good for you vs. what's the latest gimmick. (Ahem, negative calorie soda is too good to be true— obviously!)

Micro vs. Macronutrients

If you've ever fallen down a #fitspo rabbit hole on Instagram (guilty), you may have seen a lot of hashtags dedicated to "macros." Short for **macronutrient**, a macro is one of the big-picture components of your daily diet, i.e., a **carbohydrate**, **fat**, or **protein**. You rely on macronutrients to do everything. That means sitting at your desk, eating a delicious meal, kicking butt in a fitness class, binge watching a show on Netflix, and just breathing all require an intake of macronutrients. If, for some reason, your macro intake is off (marathon meeting schedule, junk food–filled road trip, etc.), you'll feel it in the form of low energy, major mood swings, and subpar performance in the gym.

Not all macros are created equal, and each possesses a different caloric profile. This means that gram for gram, carbs, proteins, and fats pack varying amounts of calories (more on those later):

- **Carbohydrates:** 4 calories per gram
- **Protein:** 4 calories per gram
- **Fat:** 9 calories per gram

Macros' counterparts in the diet are called **micro-nutrients** or "micros," which are divided into two categories: **vitamins** and **minerals**. You need these tiny guys to help fuel your cells and keep your organs healthy. Micronutrients are responsible for important functions, such as keeping your metabolism revved up and pumping blood through your entire body. If you're low on micros, you may experience decreased immune system functioning, fatigue, and a general sense of "blah" because your organs won't be able to function well on a cellular level.

Let me answer your first question before you even ask it: *Yes*, you have to eat healthy foods, even if you're taking a multivitamin and 50 other supplements that cover your nutrients! Nothing replaces getting micronutrients from food. While it's okay to take certain supplements (more on those in chapter 5), they're called "supplements" for a reason. They're meant to supplement an already-healthy diet. So don't count on taking a few daily pills to counteract a crappy diet.

Macro #1: Carbohydrates

You know carbs. You probably love them. But not all carbs love you back. (Modern romance, amirite?) Your body uses carbohydrates as its primary source of energy, and your brain depends on carbs in the form of something called **glucose** (a.k.a. **sugar**): tiny energy packets that power your cells. Whether you like it or not, you're hardwired to love and desire carbs because your cells need glucose to act out

important processes in your body, including everything from working out to just getting through the
workday.

Your body can store carb-generated glucose for only
a few days, which is why energy from carbs tends to go
fast. After you eat something that's carb-heavy, the food
gets broken down (i.e., converted into glucose) and
absorbed through your small intestine. Your body
eventually shuttles this glucose into your bloodstream,
where your cells greedily eat it up for energy.

But we can't talk about this process without
introducing a hugely important concept: **blood sugar**.
Also known as **blood glucose**, blood sugar is essen-
tially your body's currency; it's the energy your cells
need to operate and carry out just about every process
imaginable. Any time you eat, your food gets broken
down into glucose, i.e., sugar. This glucose is carried
into your cells to help them do their jobs. And just like
you work to keep your bank accounts out of the red,
your body constantly works to keep your blood
glucose in balance. If the amount of sugar in your
blood gets too high, your body has to find places to
stash the excess. If your blood sugar gets too low, you
start to feel faint and weak because your cells are
ravenously searching for energy. The amount of
glucose in your blood directly impacts your energy

levels, and it also directly influences your weight and overall health.

So what happens when you go on a carb bender? (No need to feel ashamed. Remember, you're hard-wired to love this stuff, and we've all reached for pizza or pie during hard times. Even the almighty Oprah loves bread.) When you consume excess glucose, your liver stores some of it to help regulate your blood sugar balance, which basically means that it can free up glucose down the line if it has to. This stored energy is known as **glycogen**.

But your liver's not the only place extra sweetness goes. *Um, but what happens to the rest of it?* I hear you wondering out loud, mid-bite. Sorry to be the bearer of bad news, but this might be the time to put down that bagel. Anything your liver isn't able to store turns into fat. Unfair, I know.

There are a lot of hormones at play when we talk about how your body deals with carbohydrates. One important power player is **insulin**, which is released by the pancreas. The main role of insulin is to signal cells to gather and store glucose from the bloodstream, and it's also the hormone in charge of telling your body whether that glucose is destined to be glycogen or fat. (So yeah, you want to be on real good terms with this guy.) Unfortunately, when you eat a lot of processed sugars and carbs, your pancreas releases more and more insulin. Over time, this hormone becomes less effective in your body. (Told ya you wanted to stay on insulin's good side.) This situation is known as **insulin resistance**, and it can set you up for some major health problems.

But back to that word "processed" for a sec. Processed carbs include more than just the stuff you used to get on Halloween. These are carbs that have been altered from their original forms through processes such as heating and the addition of chemicals to make them taste sweeter, last longer, or just seem yummier—as if carbs weren't yummy enough. This category of processed carbs includes everything from white bread and pastries to "sugar-free" latte syrup and coffee creamer. One vanilla latte probably won't push your insulin over the edge, but consuming these kinds of **simple/"quick" carbs** (i.e., sugars, white starches, and other carbs that your body breaks down quickly) can cause your pancreas to stop functioning over time. This can eventually result in major health issues, including obesity and diabetes.

But know this: Not all carbs or even calories are created equal. (Again, we'll talk more about the calorie thing later.) Your body and brain need carbs to function properly, so cutting them out entirely is not the way to go, unless you're ready to alienate all your friends and family with major mood swings and out-of-the-blue tantrums. Instead, you need to understand how to pick the right kinds of carbs and work on eliminating your fear of the healthy ones.

Your body takes its sweet time (pun totally intended) digesting healthy or **complex/"slow" carbs**. That means this slow-but-steady process also slows down your absorption of glucose. Examples of slow carbs include:

- Edamame
- Sprouted grain bread
- Oatmeal
- Apples
- Buckwheat
- Brown rice
- Artichokes
- Asparagus

In contrast, refined or simple/"quick" carbs are things like:

- White bread
- White rice
- Potatoes

- Jam
- Fruit juice
- Soda

These quick carbs directly impact your insulin levels and negatively affect the levels of another important hormone in your body called **leptin**. Leptin is the crucial chemical messenger that tells your brain *you're full*. (*I've never met this hormone*, you might be thinking.) Time to get acquainted. When you eat a ton of refined sugars in the form of processed breads, sweets, and snacks, leptin doesn't get adequately activated, so your brain never gets the signal that you've had enough. You keep feeling hungry, so you keep on shoveling in fluffy/gooey/sugary/carby calories.

There's another V.I.H. (Very Important Hormone) you need to be familiar with to fully understand macronutrients. You may not know it by name, but you're actually already closely acquainted with **ghrelin**. It's basically leptin's evil soap opera twin. It's the hormone that increases your appetite and is responsible for your hunger pangs. Ghrelin is primarily released in your stomach, and it signals to your brain that you're ready for food. Typically, ghrelin levels rise before you eat a meal, and they decline for about three hours after. But ghrelin regulation isn't just about *when* you eat; it's about *what* you eat. Researchers have found that diets rich in healthy carbs like whole grains (as well as good-for-you proteins) can help keep ghrelin levels low.

So back to my initial argument against cutting carbs. Have you ever tried to drastically reduce your intake of carbs or calories in an effort to lose weight? Did you somehow manage to avoid snapping at your loved ones or inadvertently sabotaging your job? Well, that's impressive. Did you instead find yourself crabby, cranky, and, above all, *starving*? Yeah, I thought so. That nightmare scenario was not your imagination. Your body is programmed to protect you from starvation, and one way it does this is to rev up ghrelin production to make sure your brain knows it needs food. (So smart, right?) Additionally, your body will turn *down* the dial on leptin production, keeping you from ever really feeling satisfied. That hormonal double whammy is what sabotages your success every time you try to convince yourself an all-egg-white diet is the perfect pre-vacation weight loss plan.

Ghrelin is like an impressionable pre-teen: It's easily influenced. Two other factors that have a significant impact on ghrelin are **sleep** and **stress**. Research shows that sleep deprivation is linked to increased ghrelin and hunger.[2] Additional studies[3] have shown that as stress levels rise, so does ghrelin. So in addition to adequately managing your macros, make sure you're getting enough good rest to keep your ghrelin under control.

Carbs Continued: Why Fiber Is Your BFF

Fiber is the holy grail of all nutrients. Fiber acts like a vacuum cleaner in your body, sucking up starches and fats and efficiently shuttling them out through the **gastrointestinal (GI) tract**. You need high-fiber foods in your diet to promote weight loss and eliminate toxins, and you need to get both kinds of the nutritional superstar: **soluble** and **insoluble**.

- **Soluble fiber:** This type of fiber is found in foods such as beans, oatmeal, nuts, seeds, and berries. A diet high in soluble fiber can reduce your risk of heart disease, diabetes, and high cholesterol. Foods high in soluble fiber accomplish this by slowing down the rate at which sugar is released into your bloodstream.

    Soluble fiber dissolves in water and coats your intestines by forming a sticky, gel-like substance that prevents your body from absorbing sugar too quickly. It also traps toxins and eliminates them from your digestive tract. This helps slow down your digestion so you feel full for a prolonged period of time. This is also the type of fiber that can help lower your blood pressure and glucose levels—good stuff all around.

- **Insoluble fiber:** This fiber is found in grains such as barley, buckwheat, and brown rice, and you'll also get a healthy dose from green, leafy vegetables. (Spinach salad, anyone?) Insoluble fiber provides bulk for your stool and reduces your risk of constipation by regulating your bowel movements.

Without both soluble and insoluble fiber, toxic waste that should be eliminated from your body stays put, accumulating in your colon. As your body holds on to these toxins, you retain fluid, feel increasingly bloated, and might start to notice the number on the scale bumping up. Filling up on fiber in the form of fruits, nuts, and whole grains is essential to keeping your body happy and your belly flat. But the fact is, if you're like most modern Americans, you're simply not getting enough. While our ancestors typically consumed almost 100 grams of fiber per day, many of us now struggle to get in just 10 to 15 grams, thanks to all those overprocessed, unhealthy meals and snacks.

The general recommendation from various health agencies is to eat about 20 grams of fiber per day. But in my book (which this happens to be), 20 just doesn't cut it. Fiber plays such a pivotal role in helping you maintain a healthy body, balanced gut, and reduced risk of obesity and diabetes (the makings of a lean and clean lifestyle) that I recommend aiming for 30 grams a day. The easiest way to stay on track with your goals is to glance at the nutrition label before you put an item in your grocery cart to see how much fiber you're actually getting. Or—bonus!—opt for whole foods found in nature, and reference the fiber guide on the opposite page.

Fiber is crucial for good health. A lot of whole foods contain both types of fiber, and if you're trying to maintain your weight, each type has important benefits. That's why it's important to diversify your diet and eat a variety of foods. You want to aim for about 30 grams or more of total fiber every day, but remember to remain mindful of how hydrated you are while you increase your intake. Too much fiber too fast can cause gas and bloating. Drink plenty of water while increasing your fiber intake, and you'll feel satiated without blowing up like a balloon.

If your diet is in serious need of a fiber overhaul, load up on these whole food powerhouses:

Fruits

- 1 cup raspberries = 8 grams
- 1 medium pear with the skin = 5.5 grams
- 1 medium apple with the skin = 4.4 grams
- 1 medium orange = 3.1 grams
- 1 medium banana = 3.1 grams

Vegetables

- 1 medium boiled artichoke = 10.3 grams
- 1 cup boiled green beans = 8.8 grams
- 1 cup boiled broccoli = 5.1 grams
- 1 cup boiled turnip greens = 5 grams
- 1 cup boiled Brussels sprouts = 4.1 grams

Grains, Cereal, and Pasta

- 1 cup cooked whole wheat spaghetti = 6.3 grams
- 1 cup cooked barley = 6 grams
- ¾ cup bran flakes = 5.5 grams
- 1 medium oat bran muffin = 5.2 grams
- 1 cup oatmeal = 4 grams

Nuts, Seeds, and Legumes

- 1 cup boiled split peas = 16.3 grams
- 1 cup boiled lentils = 15.6 grams
- 1 cup boiled black beans = 15 grams
- 1 cup boiled lima beans = 13.2 grams

Natural vs. Unnatural Carbs

Remember when I said cutting carbs was a bad idea?
I wasn't kidding. Approximately 70 percent of all the
calories you consume should come from complex,
good-for-you carbs like whole grains, fruits, and
veggies. So yes, carbs are life, but life-giving carbs =
fresh produce, grains, beans, and legumes, not Cro-
nuts and deep-dish pizzas.

Before you freak out about me bashing the good
name of the almighty Cronut, allow me to explain.
When we talk about the kinds of carbohydrates that
aren't found in nature (we generally don't see soft
pretzels and triple-stuffed Oreos growing in a garden),
we're talking about those refined/quick/simple carbohydrates. These are the notorious foods that are often
labeled "bad" carbs because they tend to have a higher
glycemic index. (In other words, they make your
blood glucose skyrocket. We'll talk more about the
glycemic index later.) These foods are converted to
sugars super quickly in your bloodstream.

If you're totally at a loss when it comes to choosing
healthy carbs, take a look at this list and shop accord-
ingly.

- **Beans and legumes:** These carbs expand in
  your stomach and provide bulk and density

while taking a longer time to digest. Because they help stabilize your blood sugar, beans and legumes are supremely healthy carbs. For those of you thinking, *WTF is a legume?* the answer is simpler than you think: It's just a plant that has a seed inside a pod. Some of my favorite legumes to add to meals include kidney beans, alfalfa sprouts, black eyed beans, pinto beans, and edamame. Legumes are considered nutritional goldmines because a small amount can keep you full, and they are slowly but easily processed in the body. Legumes are excellent sources of fiber and other important nutrients like folic acid and protein.

- **Brown rice:** This is another great option because it contains the whole rice grain, and is full of vitamins such as magnesium, B_6, and selenium.

- **Sweet potatoes:** Surprisingly, these are lower in sugar and starch than traditional potatoes. They contain high quantities of potassium, an immune-boosting mineral that can be helpful in muscle recovery.

- **Green leafy vegetables:** There's a reason kale is so hot right now. But the green guy also has

majorly nutritious cousins like cabbage, broccoli, Brussels sprouts, and asparagus.

So, see, there are plenty of good carbs out there.
Unfortunately, if you take a look at the **Standard
American Diet** (the acronym for that is literally
SAD—how sad is that?), the most common sources of
carbohydrates are foods made of processed white flour
and an alarmingly large quantity of sugar. Let's talk
about that.

Another Major Carb Subpoint: Sugar

Sugar is another type of carbohydrate, and—shocker—
our taste buds love it. Way too much. U.S. adults now
consume in excess of 30 percent more added sugar
than we did three decades ago, and researchers have
also noted that the average American consumes more
than a pound of sugar each week.[*] That's close to the
weight of a Paris Hilton purse dog. Let that sink in for
a second. (RIP, Tinkerbell!)

Over the past several decades, consumption of
sugar has only continued to increase. This influx of
refined sugars (i.e., the processed kinds found in
packaged snacks, not the naturally occurring stuff in
fruits and veggies) contributes to weight gain, obesity,

and generalized inflammation throughout the body. Your cells can't adequately process these kinds of sugars, so the only way they know how to deal is to send your insulin surging, which in turn causes fat to accumulate and deposit itself throughout your body and around your organs. These sugars are called **refined** because to bring them into existence and into your sodas and foods, manufacturers rely on a refining process to either synthesize them from naturally occurring sugars or, worse, completely manufacture them from chemicals (yum).

Back in the fat-free/low-fat/nonfat/lite era (what a dark time it was), food manufacturers packed grocery store shelves with super fake, sugar-filled products, trying to convince consumers that cutting the fat from their diets would lead to leaner physiques and better health. Then Atkins, South Beach, and the Zone came along, promoting the idea that fat isn't just necessary; it's beneficial. The real culprits, authors and various "experts" claimed, were carbohydrates, specifically in the form of sugar. While the popularity of these fad diets has waned in recent years (hallelujah!) and healthy carbohydrates are back on the table, suspicion and criticism around sugar has only grown. And there's plenty of credible evidence to back up the belief that sugar is to blame for everything from obesity to heart disease.

But when you talk about "sugar," you're not just talking about one thing, so it's important to understand some basic facts:

- "Sugar," as you know it, can be broken down into the following three types of simple carbohydrates: **sucrose, glucose,** and **fructose**. As far as your taste buds are concerned, sugar is sugar is sugar, and all varieties pack the same sweet punch and the same amount of calories per gram. But your body processes them differently.

- **Lactose** is a naturally occurring sugar found in milk and milk products. Lactose is not added sugar, but the sugar that is found in unadulterated milk.

- **Glucose** is also commonly known as blood sugar. Your body converts most carbohydrates into glucose so it can either use it for energy or store it for later. Remember, your body produces insulin in response to elevated blood glucose levels.

- **Sucrose** is chemically composed of glucose and fructose, and it's what you're most familiar with usually called table sugar. While some fruits and veggies naturally contain it, it's often added to everything from soda and cereal to ketchup and yogurt.

Added sugar doesn't have any nutrients, no matter what form it's in, so there's no **Recommended Dietary Allowance (RDA)** for it. While the **Institute of Medicine** once recommended that no more than 25 percent of your calories should come from added sugars, the **American Heart Association** is much more strict, recommending less than 100 calories of added sugar per day (about 6 teaspoons) for women, and less than 150 calories per day (about 9 teaspoons) for men.[5] This basically means the actual *required* amount of daily intake is *none*.

The **Food and Drug Administration (FDA)** recently came out with their first official recommendation, and it falls somewhere in between the other two. They say no more than 10 percent of your daily calories should come from added sugar (for adults, that means about 12.5 teaspoons, or 50 grams, about what you'd find in a can of Coke).[6]

The World Health Organization (WHO) says the 10 percent cap should exclude naturally occurring sugars in fruits, vegetables, and milk, but that people should really aim for 5 percent or less for better health.[7]

Because sugar shows up in unexpected places, it's important to understand how to identify it. If you see any of the words below on an ingredient list, you know the product you're about to eat is packing added sugar:

- Brown sugar
- Corn syrup or corn sweetener
- Fruit juice concentrate
- High-fructose corn syrup (HFCS)
- Honey
- Malt sugar
- Molasses
- Raw sugar
- Sugar
- Syrup
- Any words ending in "-ose," like dextrose, fructose, glucose, lactose, maltose, and sucrose

Let's go back to fructose because this one is probably the most confusing form of sugar because it has a mixed reputation. On one hand, it's a "natural" sugar, but on the other, it gained notoriety, particularly when it's in the form of **high-fructose corn syrup (HFCS)**, the aforementioned additive that's often used in sodas and other junk foods. HFCS is a type of adulterated corn that's been picked apart, processed, and chemically modified. It was first created because we have an abundant source of corn in our country, but over the years, experts have uncovered its harmful effects on the body. Some of the most common hiding places for HFCS are protein bars, instant oatmeal, salad dressing, pasta sauce, and peanut butter, so beware.

Most of the fructose Americans consume isn't coming from fruit. It's coming from HFCS or sucrose in packaged foods.[8] The bottom line is that you're eating way too much of this "natural" sugar—an average of 55 grams per day for adults and 73 grams for adolescents.[9] Experts such as Robert Lustig, M.D., a professor of pediatrics and an obesity specialist at the University of California, San Francisco, say this is troubling for a lot of reasons—particularly because the increase in fructose intake parallels skyrocketing rates of issues like obesity and diabetes.[10]

As I mentioned earlier, just about all of your body's cells use glucose for energy. But when it comes to fructose, only liver cells can process this. A few of the final products can be damaging. One is a form of harmful fat called **triglyceride**, which can contribute to clogged arteries and liver damage. Yet another product of fructose processing: **free radicals**, which damage healthy cells. Not to mention, too much fructose consumption is also associated with **insulin resistance**, a diabetes precursor.

When many of my patients first learn about the dangers of fructose, they immediately panic, assuming fruits should be off the table. But fructose from fruit isn't the problem. It's the amount and form of fructose you're consuming that's negatively affecting your health. When you consume fruit, you're not just getting straight sugar. You're taking in a healthy dose of fiber, which, as you know, slows down the absorption of sugar. The USDA generally recommends two cups of fruit a day, and the vitamins, minerals, and nutrients in various forms of fruit make it an important part of most diets. Observational studies have even linked increased fruit consumption with lower body weight and a reduced risk of diseases associated with obesity.[11] Foods with HFCS however generally have very little to any fiber or antioxidants.

Some fruits contain more sugar than others, so if you're concerned that you're overdoing it on fructose, you may want to stick to low-sugar options like berries (4 to 5 grams of sugar per 100-gram serving), apples (6 grams), or cantaloupe (8 grams). If you're trying to keep your sugar intake low, steer clear of high-sugar options like grapes (16 grams) and mangoes (14 grams).

I don't recommend eating more than two servings of fruits per day.

Fruit is a fantastic way to hit your sweet tooth and can be a cold and refreshing treat. Many fruits are already pre-portioned so I love that built in size guide, but some fruits can be more nutritionally dense and better for you than others, especially when it comes to sugar content.

Here are my favorite fruits that are high in fiber and lower in natural sugars:

- Apples
- Blueberries
- Strawberries
- Blackberries
- Oranges
- Pears
- Plums

Here are the fruits I tend to avoid or limit because they not only have more sugar but also sometimes have less fiber:

- Mango
- Watermelon
- Pineapple
- Grapes

- Canned Fruits
- Dried Fruits

The Glycemic Index

When you think of carbs, it's important to consider the effect they have on your blood sugar. That's the easiest way to determine if the carb you're about to inhale is healthy or not. To figure this out, you need to understand the glycemic index.

The **glycemic index** of a food is a fancy way of describing how that food affects your blood sugar. Remember: Blood sugar is your body's currency. You want your blood glucose to be high enough that it helps provide your body with energy, but not so high that you can't use all that energy and are forced to store the extra glucose as fat. If the glycemic index of a particular food is high, that food converts to sugar quickly and leads to spikes in your blood glucose levels, most likely followed by a quick drop. (Oh, hey there, mood swings, I see you.) Low glycemic foods will keep your blood sugar more stable, and they'll also keep you feeling full. (Bonus!) That's because these foods tend to be a lot denser and higher in protein and fiber, and they release glucose and energy into your bloodstream slowly so you'll avoid the roller-coaster highs and lows.

- **Low Glycemic Index Foods (55 or less):**
  - 100 percent stone-ground whole wheat or pumpernickel bread
  - Oatmeal (rolled or steel-cut), oat bran, muesli
  - Lentil or buckwheat pasta, barley, bulgur
  - Sweet potato, corn, yam, lima/butter beans, peas, legumes, and lentils
  - Many fruits
  - Non-starchy vegetables and carrots
- **Medium Glycemic Index (56 to 69):**
  - Whole wheat, rye, and pita bread
  - Quick oats
  - Brown, wild, or basmati rice, couscous
  - Banana, mango
  - Beets
  - Corn
- **High Glycemic Index (70 or more):**
  - White bread or bagels
  - Corn flakes, puffed rice, bran flakes, and instant oatmeal
  - Short-grain white rice, rice pasta, and macaroni and cheese from mix
  - White potato
  - Pretzels, rice cakes, popcorn, and saltine crackers
  - Watermelons and pineapples

Macro #2: Protein

Protein plays a pivotal role in creating a lean, clean, and healthy body. Proteins are made up of amino acids, which are the building blocks that help muscles, tissues, and other organs rebuild and repair. When you eat protein, your body breaks it down to use as a source of energy. The smaller by-products that are left over once you've processed it play a major role in many of your body's metabolic processes.

So how does all of this work? (In other words, how does last night's chicken breast become energy-boosting body fuel?) Let's start from the beginning. When you consume protein, your body releases a digestive hormone called **glucagon**. This is the stuff that encourages your body to metabolize fat. (Yasss!) But your body's not the only one stoked over the protein hit; your brain gets excited too. When it senses you've eaten a protein-packed snack or meal, it signals its command center (a.k.a. the **hypothalamus**) to tell the rest of your body you're full, and subsequently, that big ol' bread basket on the table starts to look a lot less appealing.

But how do you know if you're getting enough protein to reap the awesome benefits of fat burning and fullness? Some of you might be getting enough because thanks to all those meat-heavy diet trends spanning the spectrum from Atkins to Paleo, most Americans aren't coming up short when it comes to protein. But don't get too cocky just yet. It's not *impossible* to be protein deficient, especially if you're a vegetarian, vegan, or an athlete, or if your diet is so heavy in refined carbs that you don't have much room for protein. In fact, it can be kind of tough to get all the protein your body needs when you're on a restricted diet or you spend your days working out. It's not always easy to understand what constitutes the right amount, but a good fact to keep in mind is that the Recommended Dietary Allowance (RDA), i.e., the minimum amount you need to stay healthy, is 0.8 gram of protein per kilogram of body weight.

If you saw the word "kilogram" (or realized this formula required math) and freaked out, don't worry. There's a tool for that. The USDA has a handy calculator that allows you to figure out your needs without doing calculus (**https://www.nal.usda.gov/fnic/interactiveDRI/**). For example, if you're a 30-year-old active woman who's 5'5" and weighs 130 pounds, you'll need about 47 grams of protein a day. So what does that mean in plain English? An easy way to figure out your needs is to take half your weight in pounds and subtract 10. For example, if you weigh 150 pounds, half your weight is 75, subtract 10 = 65 grams of protein per day is what you should aim for. If you're eating a 6-ounce steak every night (which I don't recommend doing), you'll be getting close to 25 grams of protein, but most foods don't tend to carry that much, especially if you're limiting your meat intake, and it can be hard to tell if you're getting enough. That's why it's important to be aware of what your body's telling you and to recognize the following signs that you're not getting enough protein.

- **You're always on the hunt for sweets.** Protein has a lot of important jobs, but a big one is stabilizing your blood sugar levels. When you're getting enough protein, you should feel relatively stable all day long, with no major morning sugar rushes or mid-afternoon crashes. But if you're lacking protein, you might start craving candy and sweets to perk you up. While a handful of M&M's might give you a short-term boost, the surge of sugar is only going to exacerbate the ups and downs of your blood glucose roller coaster. Remedying the problem with protein in meals and snacks will keep you feeling more stable.

- **You can't focus.** You're not just depriving yourself of protein's benefits when you skimp on the nutrient; you're also affecting your ability to process carbs efficiently. Your brain runs on glucose, and protein helps ensure the carbs you're consuming are released in a steady manner. Without that buffer, you'll get bursts of mental clarity and energy, followed by periods of complete brain fog.

- **You're not progressing at the gym.** Protein feeds your muscles. If you're not getting enough, you'll start to lose muscle mass, and you can kiss any progress in the gym goodbye.

- **You're always sick.** Your immune system depends on protein to ward off bugs and viruses. If you're constantly coming down with something, there's a good chance you're not getting enough protein in your diet.

- **Your skin, hair, and nails are suffering.** Protein is referred to as the building block of cells for a reason. It's essential to keeping everything from your skin to your hair follicles strong. If you don't have enough protein, you may start excessively shedding strands, and your skin may start to crack and tear, leaving you vulnerable to infections.

THE REAL DEAL WITH PROTEIN POWDERS

If you've seen the massive containers at the gym or grocery store and are curious about protein powders, here is the breakdown on the most popular ones:

- **Whey protein:** Many people use this one after workouts because it's easily absorbed and it aids in muscle recovery after exercise. It wheys in (pun totally intended there) at about 120 calories and 30 grams of protein per serving.

- **Soy protein:** This plant-based protein is a good option for vegetarians and vegans, but it's not suitable for everyone. That's because there's some speculation that soy can actually affect estrogen levels, which may impact your hormonal health if you have a history of certain kinds of medical conditions. Soy protein contains 120 calories and 25 grams of protein per serving.

- **Pea protein:** This plant-based protein is digested slowly, so it can help curb your appetite by keeping you satiated longer. Adding one scoop to a daily smoothie can be a great dietary investment if you're trying to keep the munchies at bay. Pea protein is low in calories and high in protein, making it easier for you to achieve your daily macronutrient goals. It contains 100 calories and 23 grams of protein per serving.

- **Hemp protein:** This protein comes from the hemp plant, and it's also an excellent source of fiber. As you now know, the higher fiber content will give you a greater feeling of fullness and keep your bowels moving. Each serving of hemp protein has 100 calories and 12 to 14 grams of protein per serving.

Some of the best sources of protein include fish (salmon, trout, and herring), along with beans, nuts, and seeds. And don't forget about garbanzo beans, hemp seeds, and edamame. They're often overlooked as sources of protein, but they're good ones too. Another surprising hidden source of protein is spinach. You're probably not thinking of the leafy green as anything but a plant-based source of immune-boosting nutrients (which it is), but one cup of cooked spinach has almost five grams of protein. Chia seeds are also another great source. Adding just one ounce to your food can boost your protein intake by three to five grams.

Macro #3: Fats

Like many of you, I grew up in the era of "fat-free" everything. Fat (not to be confused with "phat," which JLo helped us recognize is universally a good thing) was considered to be the devil, and anything that contained it was shoved in the trash and kept far away from the house. If you've been programmed with fat fear, you're not alone, but it's time to wise up.

Let's get one thing straight right off the bat: There's crazy-processed artery-clogging fat, and then there's natural, plant-based healthy fat. Healthy fat has multiple amazing qualities:

- It helps enhance the flavor of your food.

- It triggers your brain to release chemicals that make you feel full.

- It aids in metabolizing certain vitamins— A, D, E, and K to be exact, and that's why these are known as **fat-soluble vitamins**.

Healthy fats help rebuild cell membranes and slow down digestion of carbohydrates. Optimal brain development and many metabolic processes all depend on fat, and so does your appearance. In fact, people who lack fat in their diets often suffer from mental fog, fatigue, dry skin, and brittle nails.

The trend toward demonizing fat still exists, which can make it difficult to get enough of the healthy stuff in your diet. Common signs that you're not getting enough fat in your diet include:

- Always feeling hungry even after adequate amounts of food
- Dry, dull skin
- Brittle nails
- Limp hair
- Frequent cravings for sugary foods

So yes, fat matters, and it's not a dirty word. It has a

meaningful place in your diet. When you start brainstorming ways to add it into your meals and snacks, think nuts, seeds, and oils. As a nutrient, fat provides nine calories per gram. That's more than double the amount provided by carbohydrates and protein, which is why a little healthy fat goes a long way.

But all fat is not created equal. Each type of fat has a different effect on the body.

Saturated fat: This fat is found in dairy, meat, cheese, and coconut oil. Saturated fat gets its name from its chemical structure. The molecule is tightly packed, a.k.a. "saturated," and it's usually solid at room temperature. Saturated fats have developed a bad reputation and been associated with cardiovascular disease, but recent studies have shown that sparingly consuming saturated fat from butter and coconut oil is not entirely bad for you. Ingesting saturated fat from refined foods and animal products, however, can contribute to heart disease and other chronic illness, so avoid these if possible. Additionally, if you are replacing butter with margarine or a butter substitute, you are ingesting a processed and chemically formulated product, so you are better off having a small amount of the butter or coconut oil.

GHEE

There's an amazingly nutritious fat that has been used for thousands of years. I consider it the health food world's best-kept secret: **ghee**. Otherwise known as clarified butter, ghee is a fantastic source of healthy fat because it contains **butyrate**.

Butyrate, or butyric acid, is a fatty acid that is a potent intestinal anti-inflammatory and can assist in rebuilding and preserving the cellular integrity of the colon and intestines. This means regular and moderate intake of ghee helps keep your gut healthy by blocking intestinal absorption of toxins. Additionally, butyrate has been shown to help regulate insulin levels.

One study with mice showed butyrate also influenced weight: Those mice that consumed butyrate became leaner and did not have as many metabolic problems.[12] Butyrate also lowered their cholesterol by 25 percent, triglycerides (fat in the blood —too much is no bueno) by 50 percent, and fasting insulin by 50 percent. In fact, over time, these mice ate less and had increased **insulin sensitivity**. Greater sensitivity to insulin is a good thing because it means your blood sugar is working effectively in the body.

Cooking with ghee instead of butter or oil is a great way to add butyrate to your diet. You can buy ghee at your local Whole Foods or natural foods store. I usually use a home-made option, but if buying, you can try Organic Valley. A little bit is all you need.

Unsaturated fat: Unsaturated fat is most often found in plant-based products like nuts, avocados, and olives. These foods have a chemical structure that has more gaps and spaces between the molecules (i.e., they're *unsaturated*), and they tend to be liquid at room temperature. Unsaturated fats are known to have a positive effect on the body. Studies have also shown that these types of fats may improve insulin levels and aid in controlling blood sugar levels.[13]

Trans fat: If you're going to fear any type of fat, fear this one. Trans fat is the most dangerous type of fat, particularly because of the way it's processed. Hydrogen is pumped into liquid oil to produce "**hydrogenated**" oil, which artificially creates trans fat. Why is this helpful for mass retailers and fast-food chains? Hydrogenated oils have a much longer shelf life than traditional oils, and the processed form allows them to be easily transported. But multiple studies have shown that trans fats increase cholesterol and promote heart disease and obesity.

The easiest way to avoid trans fat is to look at the food label. In 2006, the FDA started requiring all foods containing trans fat to list this on the label. (Exception: Any food with less than 0.5 gram per serving doesn't have to adhere to this standard.) That's why reading food labels is so incredibly important. To spot trans fats, look for words like:

- Hydrogenated
- Shortening
- Partially hydrogenated

Omega-3 fatty acids: Omega-3s are the healthy fats that just about everyone has heard of. But do you really know what they are? They're considered **"essential" fatty acids** because your body relies on them for a variety of important functions, but it can't actually manufacture them on its own. That's why you need to get omega-3s from your diet. Omega-3s are known to help reduce inflammation. Research has shown us that high levels of inflammation can contribute to low immune function and bad skin. (More on inflammation in chapter 2.)

There are three different types of omega-3s:

- **EPA** and **DHA** are found in abundance in cold-water fish (salmon, cod, and canned tuna).
- **ALA** is found in many plant sources, such as flaxseeds and walnuts. While ALAs are less potent forms of omega-3s, your body knows how to convert them to EPA and DHA, so

they're still a good source of omega-3s for vegetarians or vegans.

Oils Uncovered

Walk into your local grocery store in search of cooking oil, and you might just walk right out in frustration. There are so many options these days, and new products seem to pop up all the time. First it was vegetable oil, then olive oil, then coconut oil: Confusing much? Here's all you need to know:

Consider your cooking oils based on smoke point. The smoke point is the temperature at which the heated oil starts to smoke and the fats break down. (You know, like that time you tried to deep-fry and it smoked up your kitchen!)

Flaxseed oil: Low smoke point, meaning it doesn't handle high heat very well. It's best for dressings and dips. Great source of omega-3s but not good to use for cooking. Store this oil in the refrigerator because it can go bad quickly.

Olive oil: Medium smoke point, contains omega-9 fats and oleic acid, a component that helps our bodies to better absorb omega-3s. This oil also sensitizes cells to insulin, so it is healthier for metabolism and for fat burning. Great for cooking vegetables and meats. Not great for frying.

Sesame oil: Medium smoke point, great for cooking. Nutty flavor, good for Asian cooking. Specific taste, so not good for all-around cooking.

Safflower oil: High smoke point, good source of vitamin E, and easy to use for baking.

Canola oil: Easily available, great for cooking and sautéing. High source of monounsaturated fats, and very light flavor, so it can be used for many things.

AVOID AT ALL COSTS: Margarine and lard are the ones to stay away from. Margarine is highly processed. Lard is animal based, and it's usually extremely high in saturated fat entirely from animal sources. This makes lard highly inflammatory and challenging to cook with.

Nutrition and Diet Summary

- The body needs carbohydrates, protein, and fat. A balance of the three is what sustains a healthy body.

- Carbs can be your friend! Always look for carbs that are unadulterated and don't come in a package.

- Bread isn't dangerous, but chemically processed flour to make bread and food is what you want to avoid.

- Sugar isn't just at the candy store anymore, it is found everywhere. Look for decoys of sugar like fruit juice concentrate, malt sugar, and HFCS, and keep these out of your diet.

- Fruit isn't the enemy. It contains fiber and antioxidants, but a diet too heavy in fruits leaves less room for protein and fat, so enjoy fruits in moderation or if you need a sweet. #Naturescandy

- Fat isn't the enemy. Your cells and brain need fat to function. A little goes a long way. Avoid animal fat and trans fat. These are the bad guys.

- Protein is important in all cellular functions.

- Calculate your protein needs with the following formula: (Your weight in pounds ÷ 2)-10 = target protein grams per day.

- Protein powders can be helpful, but know what you are buying (See page 50.)

Beyond
the Nutrition
Basics

N ow that you understand the components of food, it's important to know what you're getting when you head to the grocery store or go online to order your groceries. Portions and sizes have changed dramatically over the years, and it's hard to know exactly what a real serving is. But don't be intimidated. I'll help you understand a label quickly, so you can be in and out of the store fast and never say, "I had no idea that was in there" ever again!

Making good food choices doesn't need to be very complicated. Once you understand what to look for, what to take with you, and what to toss, your shopping cart will be loaded with foods that can make you feel more energetic. What we call "food" can mean many different things, but finding and consuming real, true foods for the majority of your diet will help you sustain that lean and clean body and mind.

Decoding the Language of Nutrition Labels

For more than two decades, the nutrition label plastered on all packaged foods from chips and soda to protein bars and sports drinks has looked exactly the same. The intention of the mandatory label was always to help Americans make healthier food choices, but there's been a long-standing debate about whether the information on the label actually helps or hurts consumers. After two years of working on updates, the FDA finally unveiled a newly retooled label in 2016.

To the casual observer, not too much changed. Categories such as calories, fat, and sodium were still displayed in plain black print, and numbers including serving size, grams, and percentages were still on display. But the subtle changes to the nutrition label are a big deal. In fact, they speak to some of the recent cultural dialogue that's been happening around nutrition in America. The changes are small but significant, empowering consumers to make some better informed decisions around what they're buying and putting into their bodies. As Michelle Obama put it, "You will no longer need a microscope, a calculator, or a degree in nutrition" to figure out the nutritional value of certain foods.

By 2018, all major food manufacturers will have to change their labels to meet these updated guidelines. Look for these changes in supermarkets. Here are the top three takeaways from the new label:

- **Serving sizes:** With the old labels, the food companies got to decide what constituted a "serving." (This is why so many of us have had that awful moment of regret upon realizing a three-ounce bag of Doritos actually contains three servings.) Now labels must list realistic serving sizes and the nutrition stats that go along with them. Some experts have argued that listing these sizes will only encourage Americans to consume more, but the FDA believes forcing shoppers to confront the reality of what's in the bag, box, or wrapper will actually motivate them to eat less.

- **Calories:** The calories in a serving used to blend in with the other nutrition stats, but now the number will be required to be bigger and bolder to ensure consumers don't miss it.

- **Added sugars:** This is a category that's never been listed on the label before, and it coincides with all the recent literature and concern focused on sugar's detrimental health effects.

Now you'll be able to easily determine just how many grams of added sugar are in every product, and what percentage of your daily value you're eating in one sitting. The numbers will also help you differentiate between naturally occurring sugars found in fruit and dairy and the kinds that are added in processing.

These aren't the only changes, but they're the ones you're most likely to notice. Others include an extra column to indicate per-serving info and per-package info, reformatted labeling for packages that fall between one and two servings (20-ounce sodas, for example, will now be considered one serving, meaning you'll get the whole truth about what's inside the bottle without having to pull out your calculator), and updated percent Daily Values for sodium, fiber, and vitamin D based on medical guidelines.

Nutrition Facts

Serving Size 2/3 cup (55g)
Servings Per Container About 8

Amount Per Serving

Calories 230	Calories from Fat 72

	% Daily Value*
Total Fat 8g	**12%**
Saturated Fat 1g	**5%**
Trans Fat 0g	
Cholesterol 0mg	**0%**
Sodium 160mg	**7%**
Total Carbohydrate 37g	**12%**
Dietary Fiber 4g	**16%**
Sugars 1g	
Protein 3g	

Vitamin A	10%
Vitamin C	8%
Calcium	20%
Iron	45%

* Percent Daily Values are based on a 2,000 calorie diet. Your daily value may be higher or lower depending on your calorie needs.

	Calories:	2,000	2,500
Total Fat	Less than	65g	80g
Sat Fat	Less than	20g	25g
Cholesterol	Less than	300mg	300mg
Sodium	Less than	2,400mg	2,400mg
Total Carbohydrate		300g	375g
Dietary Fiber		25g	30g

Old label

Nutrition Facts

8 servings per container
Serving size   2/3 cup (55g)

Amount per serving

Calories   230

	% Daily Value*
Total Fat 8g	**10%**
Saturated Fat 1g	**5%**
Trans Fat 0g	
Cholesterol 0mg	**0%**
Sodium 160mg	**7%**
Total Carbohydrate 37g	**13%**
Dietary Fiber 4g	**14%**
Total Sugars 12g	
Includes 10g Added Sugars	**20%**
Protein 3g	

Vitamin D 2mcg	10%
Calcium 260mg	20%
Iron 8mg	45%
Potassium 235mg	6%

* The % Daily Value (DV) tells you how much a nutrient in a serving of food contributes to a daily diet. 2,000 calories a day is used for general nutrition advice.

New label

Portion Sizes

Raise your hand if you've ever happily eaten a whole container of something yummy, only to realize the "100 calories" on the label was in reference to one *serving*, not the whole shebang. Five servings later, you've inadvertently blown your healthy eating goals and accidentally consumed way more sugar/fat/calories/etc. than you intended.

This is something I hear from patients all the time. They're totally confused about servings, portions, labels, and numbers, and they just want to know *how much to eat* once and for all. While answers to questions about food are rarely simple, there are some good rules of thumb to know when it comes to cooking, prepping, and eating meals and snacks.

Let's first get some basic definitions in place. A portion and a serving are two distinct quantities. A *portion* refers to the amount of food you *choose* to eat (i.e., a whole candy bar/pizza/bag of chips in the example above), and many foods are packaged as a single portion to encourage you to scarf the whole thing in one sitting. A **serving** is a measured amount of food (like half a candy bar, one slice of pizza, or one ounce of chips) that's listed on a product's food label. A portion usually contains multiple servings, and according to the **National Institutes of Health (NIH)**, American portion sizes have ballooned exponentially over the past few decades, a phenomenon known as **portion distortion**.[14]

A study published in the *Journal of the American Medical Association* found portion sizes of snacks like pretzels and crackers grew by 60 percent, sodas by 52 percent, and hamburgers by 23 percent over two decades.[15] Twenty years ago, bagels were about 140 calories each and 3 inches in diameter; now they're more than twice the calories and double the size. Given those inflated portions, it's not surprising to find adult obesity rates have more than doubled since the early 1960s.[16]

Filling your plate with healthy, balanced choices is key to maintaining your weight, but if your perception of portions is totally off, you may be sabotaging your good intentions by consuming more than you really need (or even want). Understanding how to decode a nutrition label is one of the most important ways to start taking control of what you're eating. Take a typical breakfast staple like cereal, for example. You might think that by swapping out sugary options for something like Grape-Nuts, you're killing it in the healthy eating game. And with whole grains, fiber, and a handful of real, pronounceable ingredients, Grape-Nuts is a pretty wholesome choice.

But when you take a closer look at the nutrition label, you'll see that one serving is just half a cup. If you've poured yourself some cereal lately, you'll know that half a cup barely covers the bottom of the bowl. Without knowing the facts, you could potentially be consuming two or three servings in one sitting. At 210 calories a pop (*before* milk), your wholesome choice can quickly become a calorie bomb.

But reading labels is just part of the equation. Chances are, you're eating out at restaurants at least a few times a week, and entrées rarely come with nutrition labels. In these cases, it's crucial to know how to eyeball proper serving sizes so you can make sure you're not helping yourself to monster-size portions. Research shows that when you're served more, you eat more,[17] so knowing how to outsmart this mentality is key to maintaining your waistline.

I don't endorse weighing or measuring your food. This kind of micromanaging is unrealistic, and it can also breed unhealthy, obsessive thoughts. Instead, I find it really helpful to have a go-to frame of reference for some standard portion sizes. The best reference is utilizing your hand to map out portion sizes. Here's how:

- Your fist = 1 cup = a reasonable portion of cooked rice, pasta, or veggies
- Your palm = 3 ounces = a reasonable portion of meat or seafood
- Your handful = 1 ounce = a reasonable portion of nuts or dried fruit
- Two handfuls = 1 ounce = a reasonable portion of chips, pretzels, or popcorn
- Your thumb = 1 ounce = a reasonable serving of peanut butter or hard cheese
- Your thumb tip = 1 teaspoon = a reasonable serving of cooking oil or butter

Here are some other tips I give my patients that can help you avoid super-sizing your portions:

Make sure you're not thirsty. Feeling thirsty can make you think you're hungry, so stay hydrated all day long.

Fill at least half your plate with veggies. This will ensure you get tons of nutrients and filling fiber so there's less room for the unhealthy stuff.

Choose your plates wisely. Research actually

shows that choosing plates that contrast with the color of your food can help you eat less.[18] Plus, choosing smaller plates will help you estimate more realistic portions, so size down when you can.

Split your meal or save half for later. If you're eating out with a friend, order one entrée and ask for two plates. Restaurants are notorious for gigantic portions. (Hello, Cheesecake Factory!) If you're dining alone, immediately ask for half your meal to be packaged in a to-go box *as you order*. This will cut down on the possibility of succumbing to temptation. (Out of sight, out of mind.) Plus, now you have dinner or lunch for the next day!

Set the stage for a relaxed meal. Eating in a rush or while distracted can set you up to scarf more than you mean to. Step away from your desk, put away your phone, and focus on the food in front of you.

Take the time to plate your meal and portion out your snacks. A study from Cornell University found that people ate 50 percent more chips when they weren't given visual clues about portion size.[19] If you plate the food or portion out snacks, you can clearly see how much you are eating. On the flip side, eating straight from the bag or box can sabotage your efforts, so be mindful of how much food you actually plan to eat.

HOW MUCH WATER DO YOU REALLY NEED?

Let me guess. At some point, you read an article or saw a news story that cemented this "fact" in your brain: You need exactly eight glasses of water a day to be healthy and hydrated. Somehow, the myth of eight glasses spread like wildfire. But it turns out there's no real science to prove this.

What we *do* know is that the human body needs water. Why? Without water, your body would be unable to function after just a few short days. Water helps every cellular process in the body, including brain function, waste elimination (i.e., going number 1 and 2), and weight loss. Did I get your attention with that last one? That's right; your body needs water to slim down because adequate hydration helps reduce bloating, water retention, and constipation.

But what's with the eight-a-day rule? Every body is different, and your water needs depend on a lot of different factors. Here's a quick and easy way to calculate your body's H_2O needs: Take your body weight in pounds and divide the number by two. This equals the approximate number of ounces of water you would need to consume at a minimum if you were totally inactive. So if you weigh 140 pounds, you would need 70 ounces if literally all you did all day long was sit on the sofa and indulge in a *Real Housewives* marathon. Just to make it through hours of catfights and collagen-plumped lips, you'd still need to hydrate! Assuming a Bravo TV binge is not the extent of your daily to-do list, add to that original number of ounces an extra liter to account for all your daily activities and exercise. All together, the grand total could range from 2 to 3 liters per day, which is 90 to 100 ounces or 12 to 13 cups. So much for a paltry eight.

Anti-Inflammatory Foods

If you're looking for one common culprit responsible for a variety of health problems, look no further than this bad guy: inflammation. Chronic inflammation is prevalent in several common diseases. Believe it or not, it's what contributes to breakouts, bloating, and even obesity. Feeling extra fatigued, always low on energy, or constantly battling some sort of infection? Guess what's at fault. Yep: Inflammation is at it again.

In a normal immune system, when the body encounters a source of stress, such as the common cold or a cut on the finger, inflammatory signals are sent out to start the repair process. But this amazing healing process can easily get interrupted and compromised by our own actions. Example: Eating tons of junk. Foods high in refined sugars interfere with the repair process by making the immune system less effective and less capable of fighting intruders and infections quickly. This ultimately leads to chronic inflammation, and that, as you already know, can set you up for tons of long-term issues.

So what can you do about this? A lot, actually. Anti-inflammatory superfoods can help stop the cycle of chronic inflammation, improve your overall health, and boost your energy.

Another big bonus of these superfoods? Reducing inflammation in your body also leads to better skin.

That's because the redness and swelling that accompany a breakout are your body's way of telling you it's dealing with some major inflammation, both on the local level and in a general, all-over way. But you can combat this inflammation with some delicious, natural foods. Here are my favorites to add to your diet to reduce inflammation:

- **Cruciferous vegetables:** This group includes cauliflower, broccoli, and cabbage, which have all been shown to reduce inflammation because of their high content of vitamins and minerals like vitamin E, zinc, and magnesium.

  Quick Tip: Cut these veggies up on a Sunday and package them in individual containers to eat throughout the week. They make great, quick snacks when you pair them with hummus, or you can toss one of your pre-portioned servings into a stir-fry with brown rice for dinner in less than 10 minutes.

- **Nuts:** You should be going nuts for nuts. These little guys contain calcium, vitamin A, selenium, and fiber. All of these elements are potent inflammation fighters. I like to have a mix of salty and sweet to keep things interesting.

  Quick Tip: Mix a handful of almonds, walnuts,

and carob chips or dark chocolate chips to get a tasty mix. But only eat a handful once per day. It's super easy to go overboard and eat more than a single serving, but the calories and fat can quickly add up.

- **Tomatoes:** This fruit[*] contains a phytochemical called **lycopene**. Lycopene helps stimulate enzymes to break down toxins in your body.

  Quick Tip: Cooked tomatoes can pack an even bigger punch in nutrients, so don't shy away from fresh tomato sauce and soup.

- **Turmeric:** Many Asian countries began using this spice centuries ago because it possesses potent antibacterial and anti-inflammatory properties. It's most commonly found in Thai and Indian cuisines along with some Middle Eastern foods. If this type of food isn't your favorite, no problem.

  Quick Tip: Add a teaspoon to your morning shake and you'll barely taste it. You can also try adding fresh turmeric to a cup of warm almond milk. This "golden milk" is all the rage these days.

[*] I know, the fruit vs. veggie debate is always raging for this superfood, but it's true: Tomatoes are a fruit. Trust me, I too was shocked when my third grade teacher, Ms. Barkin, broke the news to me.

Organic Foods

Ah, the big O: "organic." It's become a major buzz-word in the food industry, and I can't tell you how often patients, friends, and family ask me if the recent trends are true and if we should all be going organic or bust.

Here's what we know: In testing, non-organic foods often tend to contain much higher levels of pesticides and chemicals compared to their same organic counterparts. These findings and other research have led to a detailed evaluation of the safety of produce and what we really should be eating organic.

Since 2004, the **Environmental Working Group (EWG)**, a nonprofit organization, has maintained and updated an annual **Dirty Dozen** list, which indicates the fruits and vegetables that contain the highest pesticide load. If you're trying to economize, these are the 12 items you should invest in and buy organic.

The EWG also maintains a **Clean 15** list, noting the conventionally grown fruits and vegetables with the least amount of pesticides. These are the foods that are safer to skimp on and buy conventional, because they're less likely to be burdened with toxins.

Here's the Dirty Dozen list, indicating the foods you should absolutely buy organic whenever possible:

1. Strawberries
2. Apples
3. Nectarines
4. Peaches
5. Celery
6. Grapes
7. Cherries
8. Spinach
9. Tomatoes
10. Sweet bell peppers
11. Cherry tomatoes
12. Cucumbers

And here's the Clean 15—foods you can buy conventional, guilt-free:

1. Avocado
2. Sweet corn
3. Pineapple
4. Cabbage
5. Frozen sweet peas
6. Onion
7. Asparagus
8. Mango
9. Papaya
10. Kiwi fruit
11. Eggplant

12. Grapefruit

13. Cantaloupe

14. Cauliflower

15. Sweet potato

You can try to memorize these two lists like SAT vocabulary words, but it's usually just easier to stick to this simple rule: If the fruit or vegetable has an outer layer or covering that can be removed (think banana, cabbage, onion, avocado), you don't need to go organic. If it doesn't, it's better that you invest in the organic version.

In some cases, organic foods have benefits that can make their higher dollar value worth it. By eating organic produce, you can limit your exposure to toxins because they're grown in a more controlled environment, free of pesticides and chemicals. Organic meats typically come from grass-fed animals that are often treated in a more humane way and are not fed any hormones.

One thing that can turn shoppers off from organic produce is the sometimes imperfect appearance. But remember that blemishes and bruises are a good sign that something is totally natural. You usually won't find any organic apples the size of a newborn's head.

Really, in a world of creepy supersized everything, that's pretty comforting.

I want you to understand the term so when you see organic, you can really understand what you're buying. During the 10-Day Total Body Transformation, I want you to focus on selecting organic produce and meat whenever possible because this is going to guarantee you have the fewest amount of chemicals, pesticides, and hormones being added to your body. By eliminating these, you can truly start to flush out the junk and get your body back to a leaner and cleaner state. You will also be able to truly taste clean, unadulterated food, and this can help you make better choices going forward.

Gluten: Not Really the Satan of the Food World

Gluten is a protein found in grains such as wheat, barley, and rye. It helps to make the texture of products such as bread more pliable and elastic. Lately, it's become a more popular topic than Kylie Lip Kits or unicorn lattes. Gluten is used to create different types of dough and bread products. So why has it gotten such a bad reputation? If you have a chronic condition called **celiac disease**, then you actually have an allergy to this protein and can develop a reaction that sets off your immune system and leads to severe digestive problems. After ingesting gluten, people with celiac disease can develop rashes, fatigue, stomach pain, and diarrhea. The chronic inflammation also leads to nutrient deficiencies and intestinal damage.

But celiac disease affects only a small percentage of the population. So why do so many people get abdominal cramping, nausea, headaches, and bloating after eating certain gluten-filled foods? If you find yourself feeling icky after eating breads, pastries, or pasta, you may have a sensitivity to the gluten in these items, or to certain processed ingredients or preservatives hidden in them. This kind of sensitivity is not the same as celiac disease. If you have **gluten sensitivity**, you may have some symptoms of abdominal discomfort, but those tummy problems aren't caused by an actual allergy to gluten. That's technically a good thing, but the bad news is that there's limited data on gluten sensitivity, so the possible solutions aren't quite as tangible as the ones for celiac disease. Bummer, I know.

What experts do know is that when gluten-sensitive people limit or eliminate the protein from their diets, they tend to get significant relief from their symptoms. So why did everyone and their mom start eating gluten-free? If you look at foods that are naturally gluten-free (apples, kale, spinach, quinoa), they're super healthy and they come straight from nature. When you eat these kinds of nutritious foods that don't come in a box, wrapper, bag, or other packaging, the odds are higher that these foods will also just naturally be gluten-free. (The one exception here is whole grains. If you're not sensitive to gluten, grains like whole wheat are great complex carbs chock-full of fiber, vitamins, and minerals. If you *are* sensitive, whole grain foods might trigger your symptoms.) So if you just focus on eating a natural, nutritious diet, you may be tricked into thinking it's the lack of gluten that's changing your gut, but it's really just the fact that you're filling up on unprocessed, good-for-you foods and less junk.

One big caveat to keep in mind if you are going to go gluten-free, however: The term *gluten-free* is not a free pass to go buckwild and #treatyoself to all the things. Loading up your grocery cart with gluten-free cookies doesn't automatically make you a health nut. In reality, most gluten-free pastries, chips, and breads tend to have extra sugar or fillers that make them pretty unhealthy. So if you're faced with the choice between a gluten-free muffin or a regular muffin, the answer is pretty simple: You should probably skip them both and grab an apple.

White Isn't "Tite"

White foods sure look clean, so they must be as pure as the driven snow, right? Um, wrong. White flour is the by-product of a long, unnatural, and chemically driven process. I know you may be surprised by this (and by the fact that I brought back the word "tite" in this section title. Clearly, I miss the '90s). Despite the overwhelming temptation of the restaurant breadbasket, white flour and the foods created from it (all that yummy, squishy bread) are extremely unnatural and harmful to your body.

Here's why: Wheat is composed of three parts: the **bran**, **germ**, and **endosperm**. The bran is the outer covering of the grain and contains the most fiber. The germ is the next layer toward the center and is a concentrated source of important nutrients. The endosperm is the starchy part in the middle of the wheat plant. While there are some nutrients in here, it's mostly just a big ol' source of carbs. So guess what white flour contains? Yup, all those wholesome parts are eliminated in processing, and what you're left with is a bunch of fluffy, barely nutritious, carby endosperm (which somehow doesn't sound quite as tasty).

Once the flour has been processed at a high temperature, it's bleached and treated with chemicals like chlorine. Yes, you read that right. That's the same chemical added to swimming pools to kill bacteria. This turns the flour into a very clean and white product. Unfortunately, during this process, the wheat's not just getting a swimming pool treatment, but its healthiest parts are stripped away and replaced with gross chemicals that you eventually ingest into your body. As if that weren't bad enough, without the fiber to temper the impact on your digestion, white flour products quickly bump up blood sugar and insulin levels.

But take heart: Not all wheat is so Frankenstein-y. True whole wheat flour contains all three parts of the wheat grain, giving it that natural brown hue and making it high in nutrients, including fiber. However, beware and always read ingredient labels. Some wheat bread is also adulterated and bleached, so be on the lookout for those evil words, "high-fructose corn syrup (HFCS)," "bleached," or "enriched."

A Word on Coffee

Many of us can't seem to function without that morning cup of joe, but the way most Americans drink our coffee is far from the version that has health benefits. If you're a "creamer with a dash of coffee" type, you're simply ingesting tons of sugar and eliminating the health benefits of coffee. Coffee also contains—and you're not gonna like this—a hormone-altering substance: *caffeine*! Caffeine is amazing for alertness and energy, but it often suppresses your appetite, and this initial suppression is frequently followed by ravenous hunger that's occasionally insatiable.

Before you get super riled up and aggressively protective of your morning latte, listen. I get it. I have two toddlers who wake up randomly in the middle of the night, unexpectedly and often, and I still need to be bright-eyed for patients, work, and on-camera segments, so sometimes coffee calls my name too. But every time I pour a big cup and add in the creamer, I regret it. When I take a moment to listen to my tired body, it's not the coffee I'm really craving, but the warm, sugary drink I concocted out of it. Sometimes I win, but sometimes coffee wins, and its victory is usually followed by a less-than-healthy breakfast at 11 a.m. and a lot of trips to the bathroom. So, my advice is to try your best to avoid large cups of coffee, switch to decaf, and drink it black. And remember that a true cup of coffee is only six to eight ounces, not a venti or trenti (Have you heard of this size? I hadn't either!) or any other super-sized option.

Is Milk Bad for You?

Back to the '90s for a second. Remember the tagline of that decade was "Got milk?" In the '80s, it was "Milk: It Does a Body Good." And before that, kids across America were encouraged to gulp tall glasses of it along with every meal, no matter how unappetizing the pairing seemed.

For the better part of the past century, you've been told that dairy is what strong bones and healthy bodies are made of. You've seen everyone from Martha Stewart to the Backstreet Boys sporting milk mustaches (it was 1998, so you know...). But as time goes on and new research emerges, it is becoming more and more clear that the case for dairy consumption is much more complex, nuanced, and controversial than many of us realized. Before celebrities and lifestyle experts began singing the praises of a gluten-free lifestyle, "dairy-free" was the dietary restriction du jour, and many people began self-identifying as "lactose intoler-ant." But what does that label really mean?

Let's start with what milk is actually made of. Milk contains a sugar called **lactose**. In order for your body to digest this sugar, you need an enzyme called **lactase**. Babies generally have this enzyme in spades; after all, their diets are made up exclusively of breast milk or milk-like formula. Adults, however, theoretically don't need the enzyme to process their nutrients, so lactase production can slow down with age. Without adequate amounts of it, however, milk products are not digested properly, resulting in all sorts of not-so-fun symptoms like nausea, gas, and diarrhea.

In addition to lactose, milk contains a protein called **casein**. While your body doesn't require a special enzyme to process casein, many of us have a hard time digesting it, resulting in symptoms like those listed above, plus allergic reactions like hives and wheezing.

Seventy-five percent of the world's population has some form of lactose intolerance in addition to the abnormal digestive symptoms caused by casein. While this number is staggering, it's not entirely surprising. Think about it: Humans are the only mammals who regularly consume *other* mammals' milk. It makes some sense that issues could arise from this unique kind of interspecies dietary choice.

Some experts believe that drinking milk beyond

adolescence is associated with an increase in a specific hormone called **insulin-like growth factor,** or **IGF-1**. This hormone helps your body develop muscle and bone, and it triggers the release of other growth factors your body requires during your formative years. Cows make IGF-1 too. The FDA allows farmers to give cows something called **recombinant bovine growth hormone (rBGH)**—a synthetic hormone that increases a cow's milk production. It's been banned in Canada and throughout Europe. One potential problem with this hormone is that it actually increases levels of IGF-1.

While this sounds like an efficient way to keep the dairy industry humming, artificially stimulating milk production can clog cows' milk ducts, leading to infected udders, otherwise known as mastitis. If you're squeamish, you may want to skip ahead because mastitis causes pus and blood to enter the milk supply. If you're still able to keep your lunch down after reading that, then how about this unsavory fact: Cows with mastitis are often given antibiotics to treat the condition, and that medication goes right into their milk supply—and right into your milk carton. This can lead to unnecessary antibiotic exposure and resistance, which is a serious problem that can eventually lead to the development of untreatable superbugs.

High levels of IGF-1 in cows may have other

serious implications for milk-drinking humans. Some research shows that when IGF-1 levels are at the high end of normal, they may influence certain kinds of cancers to develop. This correlation is not entirely understood, but research continues to grow on the subject.

Those who argue for consuming dairy also have a few good points. After all, milk contains three majorly important nutrients: calcium, vitamin D (when fortified), and potassium. Because milk and other dairy products are a pretty palatable way for many people to get enough of these nutrients, the USDA recommends two to three servings per day.

But scientists are starting to poke holes in the theory that the calcium in dairy products actually builds and protects strong bones. A 2014 study published in the *British Medical Journal* found that higher milk intake was actually associated with higher incidences of bone fractures in women and higher mortality rates in both men and women.[20] And it's hard to ignore the fact that countries with virtually no milk consumption (like many places in Asia) have low rates of bone fractures.

Confused? I don't blame you. Here's my recommendation: If you like milk, it's not a crime to have it, but you should always choose an organic, non-rBGH (sometimes abbreviated as **rBST**) option, and you

certainly shouldn't be drinking two to three glasses
of it, no matter what the government recommends.
Especially because drinking multiple cups is more
likely than not to lead to gas, bloating, and lethargy—
whether you "officially" have lactose intolerance
or not. To avoid these issues, and more, keep to as little
milk as possible.

To Soy or Not to Soy

The safety and efficacy of soy is a topic of great debate
in the medical community. The controversy stems
from the fact that soy contains **phytoestrogens**, or
plant-based estrogens. When these enter the body,
they can attach to estrogen receptors, but it's unclear if
they activate or block these receptors. Some experts
believe they activate these receptors, exacerbating
estrogen-dependent health conditions like **polycystic
ovary syndrome (PCOS)**. Other experts believe this
isn't the case at all and that soy can be healthy and
protective against chronic illness and cancers.

If you look at research from Asian countries
where soy consumption is consumed in high quantities, the rates of cancer are extremely low. This would
indicate that soy consumption could be protective. In
the United States, however, soy is largely consumed

in adulterated, or modified and non-fermented, forms. When Japanese women in one study traditionally consumed soy, they tended to have the lowest rates of breast cancer. When these women were then given a traditional Western diet, their risk of cancer increased.

There's a lot we all have left to understand about soy. For now, steer clear of products that have words like "soy protein isolate" or "fractionated soy" on the label, and don't get your soy in a super-processed form like in a hot dog, patty, or sausage. So far, there's no long-term research on how these forms of soy can affect the body, so it's best to stick to naturally occurring forms like edamame and tofu.

If you really can't quit the idea of dairy, you may want to consider an alternative to cow's milk. But some of these "healthy" swaps have some hidden health pitfalls too.

Cow's Milk Alternatives

- **Soy milk:** Taking heed of the info above, you may want to try swapping in soy for traditional milk because it contains B vitamins and folate. But soy milk tends to be low in calcium, and—depending on the preparation—can be loaded with sugar, especially if it's flavored. It may also aggravate gas and bloating if you have a sensitive stomach.

- **Almond milk:** This super-low-calorie beverage can be a good option, but it's also notoriously low in protein; that's because one cup of almond milk actually contains only four or five whole almonds. But if you like a nutty flavor and less natural sweetness, you may want to give this one a try.

- **Rice milk:** Rice milk has a naturally sweet flavor, but that's because it has more carbs and sugar than regular milk, not to mention less protein (just one gram per 100-calorie cup).

- **Hemp milk:** Hemp seeds are a good source of omega-3 fatty acids and may be beneficial for cardiovascular health, and one cup of hemp milk is just 70 to 100 calories. Although it has only two grams of protein per serving, it has a thicker, creamier texture than other milks, which some people prefer.

- **Coconut milk:** Coconut milk has more saturated fat than the other types of milks, but it works well in coffee and cereal because it's richer in taste and texture. One cup has 50 to 100 calories and one gram of protein.

(continued on page 92)

BELLY FAT

One of the most bothersome (albeit common) problems plaguing my patients is an issue they usually consider cosmetic and I consider dangerous: belly fat. Most women are less than thrilled at the prospect of sporting a spare tire around their waist, but many find that no matter how disciplined they are in their eating or exercise, they can't shed the fat around their middle.

This extra padding isn't just a superficial concern, and when I hear it's a chronic problem, I pay special attention. That's because abdominal or visceral fat is way more hazardous to your health than the kind of subcutaneous fat you can see and grab. Visceral fat sits way down between your abdominal organs, and too much of it has been linked to everything from cardiovascular disease to type 2 diabetes—and even breast cancer.[21]

Hormones and genetics largely influence where you accumulate fat, so you can't necessarily diet or exercise your way to long, lanky limbs if you're naturally a curvy pear shape. That's not to say healthy habits aren't important. If you're overweight, a balanced diet and regular workout plan can definitely help, but no amount of sit-ups can correct a hormonal imbalance.

There are a few potential hormonal causes for excess abdominal fat.

- **Too much estrogen:** Excess estrogen can accumulate in your body for a variety of reasons. It can lead to a host of hormonal symptoms, including intense PMS, low libido, depression, and—you guessed it—increased belly fat.

- **Too much insulin:** By now you've learned insulin's job is to process sugar in the bloodstream. Eating too many processed carbs and sugary snacks can cause your insulin to skyrocket, leading to insulin resistance or **metabolic syndrome**. Many people with this have increased abdominal fat.

- **Too much cortisol:** The hormone **cortisol** has gained a reputation for being an instigator of belly fat accumulation. Otherwise known as the stress hormone, cortisol is what your adrenal glands pump out when you're in **fight-or-flight** mode, meaning something (real or imagined) is threatening your well-being, and you have to either fight it or run as fast as you can. Your body doesn't know the difference between a car speeding toward you or a low balance in your bank account. As far as your body's concerned, both scenarios are stressful, and both require an output of cortisol for survival. But if you're chronically stressed (which many of us are), the constant flood of cortisol will lead to stored fat around your abdomen. There's plenty of research to support this, including a Yale study that found stress may cause excess abdominal fat in otherwise slender women.[22]

Here's how to combat belly fat:

- **Keep your stress in check.** Too much stress leads to too much cortisol, and as you now know, excess cortisol is a major cause of abdominal fat. Consider incorporating yoga, meditation, or other calming practices into your life.

- **Get enough sleep.** One study in the journal *SLEEP* found that less than five hours of sleep a night was associated with increased BMI and abdominal fat in people younger than 40.[23]

- **Quit smoking.** In case you needed one more reason, research shows that smoking increases the risk of metabolic syndrome and diabetes, as well as the risk for greater abdominal fat and insulin resistance.[23]

Healthy Dairy

Don't get me wrong; I'm not entirely anti-dairy. Yogurt is the one product I definitely encourage you to consume regularly. That's because the bacteria in it are extremely beneficial to your overall health, particularly within the GI tract.

When you're going to the supermarket to buy yogurt, it's important to know what to look for. I recommend buying yogurt in larger-size containers instead of in individual servings. They tend to have less fillers, and they are a better value. Skip the skim milk version and choose 2 percent or higher. Nonfat yogurt can sometimes have added sugar to compensate for the lack of fat or flavor. Plus, the natural fat will help you feel fuller with less and leave you satisfied longer. And make sure you avoid fruit flavors and just stick to the plain stuff. If your only option is the "fruit on the bottom" variety, eat the actual yogurt and leave that "fruit" where it is.

As for cheese, some days I can't live without it! But similar to my views on milk, I try to keep this to a minimum in my diet. I want to encourage you to try to keep your cheese consumption low because most commercially sold cheese contains fillers, color additives, and a lot of processed junk. If you see things like potato starch on your shredded cheese packet, it is best to leave that bad boy at the store.

All Calories Are Not Created Equal

If you or someone you know has ever tried to lose weight, you've probably become intimately familiar with **calories**. I'd venture to say that at any given moment, anyone on a restrictive diet can rattle off the calorie count in everything from a tablespoon of ketchup (19) to a pint of Ben & Jerry's Half Baked (1,080, but who's counting?).

This isn't surprising, because we've all been fed the same idea over and over: Weight loss is simply a matter of "calories in, calories out." This rule of thumb isn't entirely wrong, but it's not entirely right either. What's definitely not right is the fear so many people have around calories themselves, going out of their way to avoid them at all costs, sipping diet sodas and snacking on artificial, low-cal protein bars. Calories *aren't* the enemy. You just have to understand how they work.

First thing's first: What is a calorie? The definition may be more mundane than you think. A *calorie* is the amount of energy needed to raise the temperature of water. It's just a unit of energy. That's it. The same way your car needs gas to power your commute, your body needs energy in the form of calories to do everything. And I do mean everything. When you restrict calories, your body senses a huge deficit of power and energy because calories help us survive.

Even if you spent the day lying in bed, engaged in a serious Netflix binge-a-thon, your body would still need a minimum number of calories to keep your organs functioning optimally. This minimum amount is your **resting metabolic rate (RMR)**, and it varies from person to person, depending on age, sex, muscle mass, and weight. It's what you need to get by, but it's not the amount you need to live. Moving around and being a busy person requires additional energy, and that means additional calories.

But here's the truth that foils so many people's best weight loss intentions: Not all calories are created equal. Living in a diet-centric universe, you're led to believe that 100 calories is 100 calories. That's why you now see so many cute, "snack-sized" packages of processed foods on grocery store shelves these days. But while fat, fiber, sugar, and protein all contain calories that can be used for energy, they're all pro-cessed at different rates. That's because their caloric density varies widely.

Caloric density refers to the average number of calories per gram of a certain food. For example, foods like vegetables that are low in calories tend to be high in water and low in fat. So 50 calories of spinach will look very different from 50 calories of ice cream, which is calorically dense. Here's a refresher on the amount of calories per gram in each macronutrient:

- Carbohydrates: 4 calories per gram
- Protein: 4 calories per gram
- Fat: 9 calories per gram

This means you'll feel very different after eating 200 calories of quality protein versus 200 calories of simple carbs. While the former will keep your blood sugar stable and your appetite satiated, the latter can actually make you even hungrier. And they're both 200 calories.

Here's how this plays out in the real world: Imagine you had the choice between two lunch options. Option A is a balanced 500-calorie meal, consisting of lean protein, whole grains, vegetables, and healthy fat. Option B? Two Krispy Kreme Chocolate Iced Glazed Doughnuts with sprinkles.

Now, if you're coming at this decision from the "a calorie is a calorie" perspective, you might just throw caution to the wind and go for option B. But think back to our initial discussion about nutrients, insulin, and blood sugar. When you indulge in option B, those doughnuts hit your system hard. With 46 total grams of sugar and just 2 (two!!) grams of dietary fiber, the doughnuts will cause your gut to quickly soak in all the glucose and fructose it can, sending your blood sugar and insulin skyrocketing. This chain reaction will subsequently block your production of leptin, so that feeling of fullness you'd expect to get after a meal just won't come. Combine that bottomless pit sensation with the activation in your brain's pleasure center, and you'll likely be starving shortly after polishing off the second doughnut.

If option B becomes your go-to lunch choice, you'll see a lot more problems pile up over time. The mega doses of sugar will lead to consistently elevated insulin levels, eventually creating a spare tire around your tummy that's not only *not* cute but also dangerous. And while those doughnuts are rich in calories, they're void of any nutrients, and they'll prime your palate to crave super-sweet, sugary treats. Anything less will taste like cardboard, perpetuating the vicious cycle of seeking out/consuming/seeking out processed junk.

But let's say you opted instead for nutritious, balanced option A. You'll consume tons of fiber thanks to the whole grains and vegetables, and the protein and fat will keep you satiated and energized. You'll sidestep the food coma that usually follows a junk food binge, and you'll absorb vitamins and nutrients that will improve the appearance of your skin, hair, nails, and more. Best of all, these micronutrients will actually protect you from serious diseases, balance your hormones, and keep your gut in top shape.

The bottom line here is that calories are units of measurement. They're not the be-all-end-all determinant of what makes a food choice healthy. It's the type of calorie that matters. Research backs this up. In a study that examined the correlation between calories, sugar, and diabetes, scientists discovered that adding 150 calories to participants' diets did little to increase the risk of diabetes—unless those 150 calories were from one specific sugary source. When the increase came from soda, the participants' risk of diabetes went up exponentially.[25] Still think a calorie is a calorie?

The Truth about Diet Soda

It's cold, it's refreshing, and hey—it's diet! What's not to love, right? By now, you've probably learned that I have a habit of debunking some big-time health myths, and this is a biggie. Sorry, ladies: Diet soda is not your friend.

You now understand why added sugar is unhealthy and even dangerous. High consumption of sugar triggers leptin and insulin resistance, which ultimately leads to weight gain. So it's perfectly understandable why you'd sink your faith into a sugar-free substitute for your favorite treats. After all, it's logical to think that since diet soda or artificial sweeteners have no sugar, they must be safe. Unfortunately, these options are even worse. Say *what?*

It's shockingly true: Diet drinks can be even more hazardous to your health than regular soda. That's because in lieu of sugar, diet soda contains pounds and pounds of artificial sweeteners and chemicals. Those fake additives confuse your brain by disrupting normal signals that are usually responsible for gauging the sweetness of a food or beverage. In fact, a University of Texas study found that over 10 years, people who drank diet soda had a significantly greater increase in their waist circumference compared to non-drinkers.[26] Another 2014 study found that overweight and obese adults who drank diet beverages consumed more calories overall than those who drank regular, sugar-packed sodas.[27] How is that even possible? It turns out that those super-potent artificial sweeteners can trigger a more intense activation of the reward centers in your brain as a result of their extremely sweet taste. Over time, your ability to sense sweetness is blunted, totally screwing up your hunger signals and hormone secretion.

There's more bad news when it comes to these carbonated chemical concoctions. Recently, a study in the journal *Nature* showed us that artificial sweeteners can also affect your gastrointestinal bacteria and can lead to insulin resistance and obesity.[28] Sweeteners containing **aspartame** (once sold as NutraSweet) also have been known to break down into by-products of formaldehyde.[29] (Yeah, the same stuff used as a preservative in *funeral homes*. Unreal, right?) And if you've been led to believe that Splenda is somehow a more natural version of fake sugar, consider this. A 2016 study found the stuff inside those cute little yellow packets was associated with increased incidences of cancerous tumors in mice.[30]

Believe it or not, I was a die-hard Diet Coke and Coke Zero fan until a few years ago. I'm not going to sugarcoat it. (ha...ha?) It was a tough habit to kick. But I used a few of the alternatives that follow to really get soda out of my system for good. If you're looking for some healthy, hydrating alternatives, here are my best recommendations:

Plain water: Okay, maybe it's not the sexiest suggestion, but plain old water really is the best source of hydration, and it's the ultimate way to feel leaner and cleaner. Always have a water bottle with you that you can refill. This helps you meet your daily water goals and can ultimately lead to weight loss.

Sparkling water: This has the same cold and

bubbly taste as soda, without the calories, sweeteners, and junk. You can also get naturally flavored varieties, which help fulfill that craving for something tasty. My favorite brands are La Croix and Perrier, but I've also heard rave reviews from friends who own a SodaStream, the machine that also allows you to make your own sparkling water.

Tea: This is a great alternative to soda, and it's loaded with antioxidants. Tea can be enjoyed hot or cold, and many varieties contain caffeine, which many soda drinkers crave. But don't be fooled by some of those fancy bottled iced teas. Always check the sugar content and make sure there are no added sweeteners or artificial flavoring.

Kombucha: Kombucha is a fermented beverage that is made of tea and fruit. Kombucha has a fizzy taste, and it will hit your soda spot without giving you tons of artificial junk. Bonus! It's also an excellent source of **probiotics**, the beneficial bacteria that keep your gut happy and healthy.

Beyond the Nutrition Basics Summary

- Nutrition labels can work to your advantage, but you have to **read** them!

- Retrain your body by plating out **one** serving of foods you commonly eat. This will teach you exactly how much you should be aiming for. A serving isn't as big as we think. This change alone can be your most powerful diet overhaul.

- We all need water. Lots of it! More than we need coffee (gasp), wine, and soda. Drinking your daily requirement of water is an easy way to get started on a healthy journey.

- Organic is important for some foods. If a fruit or vegetable has an outer covering, you don't need to buy organic, but if it doesn't, it's best to select organic. Meat and dairy are **very** important things to buy organic. This eliminates chemicals, hormones, and preservatives.

- White flour is not naturally occurring and strips all of the nutrients out. Avoid it.

- Calories aren't all created equal. The type of calories matters more than the number.

- Dairy can be confusing. In many people, it causes gas and bloating. Keep cow's milk and cheese to a minimum. Yogurt is the exception because it contains powerful probiotics and bacteria to help rebuild a healthy stomach.

- Diet soda isn't doing your diet any favors. The artificial sweeteners trick your brain and interfere with hormones and chemical signals. This makes you fatter over time and chronically unsatisfied.

3

Exercise

Exercise always does a body good, but I'm not going to just tell you that, I will show you why you need exercise in your life! I cannot survive without it. Not just for weight control, but even for mind control. Exercise is one of the few non-pharmacologic ways of releasing the same chemicals in the brain as antidepressant medications. That means if you exercise for 20 minutes, the short-term benefits are as good as or better than taking a medication to boost your mood. Exercise also helps with maintaining a stable weight, can calm anxiety and stress, and even help you sleep better.

Being an Exercise Guinea Pig

I'm about to let you in on a major, life-changing secret: the workouts I recommend for real, lasting results. Ready? Here it goes: The best exercise for your body is the kind you will actually do.

Okay, I know that's kind of a non-answer to the question of which workouts will get you leaner, fitter, and feeling amazing, but it's the truth. To reap the many (many, many) benefits of exercise, you have to commit to a realistic, sustainable regimen that you won't dread/completely avoid doing.

Busting your booty and sweating to get your tail in shape are important components of getting leaner and cleaner. Exercise is also known to reverse the aging process, improve your skin, and boost your mood without chemical help. As if those weren't enough great reasons to get moving, exercise has also been proven to help you get to sleep faster and stay asleep longer. Remember this: More often than not, you're just a workout away from improving your mood. That means that even if you throw out all the amazing ways exercise supports weight loss/maintenance and physical fitness, it's still an absolutely essential component of a healthy life and attitude.

When it comes to staying active, I'm a huge fan of trying new workouts. When I first moved to Los Angeles, it wasn't the sunny weather and palm trees that totally captivated me (although those things definitely didn't hurt). It was the amazingly fit, lean, and healthy bodies I saw all around me. I wanted to know what kept Angelenos in such great shape, so I made it a hobby to try tons of different workouts. I even had a group of girlfriends who came with me to road test new classes. We tried spin, barre, hot yoga, Pilates, and the list goes on. You name it; we tried it.

Becoming a fitness guinea pig helped me learn what I like and, more importantly, what I don't like. For example, I discovered that you can't pay me enough to go to a barre class; I just get way too bored and restless. Despite the popular opinion and millions of barre devotees, I don't take those kinds of classes, and I never want to hear someone tell me to "tuck, tuck, tuck" again. But that's just me! Barre might be the best thing that's ever happened to you. What makes you want to run, stretch, and sweat (and what makes you just want to run away screaming) might be different than me.

Among all the various workouts I tried, I discovered three that really changed my exercise game. These three workouts are backed by science, applauded by trainers, and used by celebrities everywhere. They've truly changed my body and the bodies of many of my patients. Curious to learn more? I thought so.

Workout #1: Pilates and the Megaformer

I have my gorgeous, lean, and strong friend E.J.
to thank for introducing me to the Megaformer, a
special kind of machine that takes Pilates to the next
level. E.J. has always had flat abs and killer arms. When
we first started talking about workouts, she was super
honest about how she got in shape.

"This workout is no joke," she told me. "It's so
efficient, and it's hard as hell. I did it for a while, and
when I went back home, people said I looked different."

And I knew she meant *good* different, not the kind
of "hmm…she looks *different*" often associated with a
few extra pounds or a tragic new haircut.

During this time, I was really into running, so I
thought trying her recommendation would be an easy
little break from the treadmill. I could not have been
more wrong. I barely made it through my first class.
Most Megaformer workouts are done in a class setting
at a studio. The instructors walk you through the
workout while you do the moves on the Megaformer
machine. The Megaformer changed my body and my
life—seriously! It's a more intense version of the
Pilates reformer machine. It was invented by Sebastien
Lagree, an LA fitness guru who truly perfected the

concept of resistance exercises, combining them with traditional Pilates moves. To find a Lagree fitness studio near you, you can go to LagreeFitness.com.

The Megaformer was created to harness the true power of the body. As you go through each exercise, you'll notice this routine tones your muscles, and it also helps you gain mental strength and stamina. That's because pushing through the moves requires you to embrace the "mind over matter" concept. Megaformer and Pilates reformer classes focus on building a strong core by recruiting your abs during each workout. The results are lean oblique muscles, tighter thighs, and a perkier butt. By regularly pushing through a session, you'll increase your flexibility, coordination, endurance, and overall strength. And chances are you'll eventually walk away with a slimmer waistline—not a bad bonus.

The physiology of this workout focuses on your **slow-twitch muscle fibers.** Your muscles are made up of multiple fibers that are strung together to create one larger muscle. These fibers are cells that are specialized to generate power and muscular contraction, which creates movement. Your skeletal muscle can be divided into two types of muscle fibers: **slow-twitch** and **fast-twitch**. The fast-twitch fibers are the ones that power super-short, explosive sprints, while the thinner, longer slow-twitch muscles are what keep you going during a marathon. Each movement on the Megaformer is designed to focus on those slow-twitch fibers and make you get to a point of muscle failure, meaning the point when your muscles can no longer move or continue to contract. This is a pivotal point where you begin to see your muscles change, and you'll notice them grow leaner, longer, and stronger.

In my opinion, the best way to achieve this muscle transformation is by taking your Pilates routine off the mat and onto a machine. While mat Pilates classes do help you work out without any additional tools, the machine helps isolate the muscles more effectively. Many gyms and studios offer classes on a machine called a reformer or Megaformer that uses resistance to whip you into shape while keeping you in proper alignment. By regularly doing workouts on the reformer, you start to overcome things that may be holding you back in your fitness routine and in your life.

The Megaformer allows you to take a traditional Pilates-based workout and isolate, sculpt, and chisel your body. The machine and workout were founded on the principles of Pilates to help strengthen your core muscles and lengthen and tone your body. It's super tough. I've seen big-muscled NBA players struggle during this workout. But the Megaformer or any kind of reformer is also a smart way to get your workout in because the machines prevent and protect against back injuries while improving your posture. By holding poses against resistance and engaging multiple muscle groups, you can achieve maximum caloric burn. These workouts are also a great option for someone who doesn't want high impact on their joints or is struggling to work out because of a prior injury.

To put it in perspective, here's what Sofia Vergara had to say about the Megaformer: "The workout is really intense and works out so many muscles at the same time. I love it and hate it." When *Modern Family*'s Gloria talks, we listen. And if Sofia's body isn't enough to get you interested, here are several other celebrities who swear by the Megaformer:

- Courtney Cox
- Brooke Burke
- Megan Markle
- Alessandra Ambrosio

You can't replicate this workout at home. Even going to a class once a week could help change your body and make you stronger.

Workout #2: Boot Camp and HIIT

The other workout I live by is boot camp. The first one I went to was Barry's Bootcamp in West Hollywood, and it left a lasting impression. This type of boot camp combines **high-intensity interval training (HIIT)** with an upbeat environment. Boot camps can burn anywhere from 700 to 1,300 calories per session, depending on your weight and effort level. The workout combines bursts of high-intensity moves followed by short periods of lower-energy activity.

While you might be familiar with the more glamorized side of this workout (at this very moment, one or more Kardashians may be talking about her morning HIIT session), boot camps are *intense*. They were originally used in the military, where recruits train under rigorous conditions for hours at a time and go through a series of exercises with minimal breaks. Boot camp workouts are built on a few universal themes, including strength, endurance, and mental confidence, and they incorporate tons of HIIT training.

HIIT exercises are designed to encourage you to work out at your maximum effort level, allowing you to blast calories in a short period of time. HIIT is the absolute Mac Daddy (or is it Daddy Mac?) of calorie burning because these short periods of activity create metabolic disturbances (a good thing that helps you burn fat) much more efficiently than traditional exercises while simultaneously helping to increase muscle strength.

HIIT workouts also improve endurance because the exercises are designed to continuously improve your ability to work out for longer periods of time while building up muscle and burning calories. A combination of interval training has been shown to burn fat more effectively than longer, lower-intensity exercises. How many times have you seen people just cycling away at the gym on a stationary bike or zoning out on the elliptical while reading the latest US Weekly cover to cover? You could log two hours on either of these machines, and you *still* wouldn't burn as many calories as you would in a 30-minute HIIT workout. The other benefit to HIIT training is that it can be modified for just about anyone, so no matter your skill level, you can do a HIIT workout.

So why does HIIT whip you into such great shape? Whether you realize it or not, your body continues to burn calories for one to two hours after a workout. This period of time where you see caloric burn post-workout is called the **EPOC** or **excess post-oxygen consumption** period. During EPOC, your body's trying to get back to its pre-exercise state. In order to do that, it has to consume more oxygen than it normally does. This consumption of extra oxygen also requires extra energy (i.e., calories). That means that even after a tough workout, you can continue to burn calories long after you finish your last squat or burpee.

Science suggests HIIT workouts ensure major post-exercise payoff. One study demonstrated that after a HIIT workout, the EPOC increased up to 15 percent.[31] According to another study, after two weeks of HIIT, subjects' endurance had increased almost 60 percent.[32] In short, HIIT keeps your body in a higher fat-burning zone for the 24 hours after you work out, and the constant hustle in boot camp classes really amps up your endurance. What's not to love?

If you're short on time or into more minimalistic routines, HIIT-heavy boot camps may still be for you. Many offer the opportunity to use weights and resistance bands according to your skill level. Big-time bodybuilders can work with higher resistance, and first-timers and newbies can still get an amazing workout without much resistance at all.

This also makes these types of workouts convenient because you barely need any extra accessories. In many cases, your body weight alone is enough to get you seriously sweating. The workouts are also extremely efficient. In a short amount of time (anywhere from

30 to 45 minutes), you can work every single part of your body to exhaustion. And maybe the biggest boot camp benefit? You'll be surrounded by other people pushing themselves to the max, meaning you can't help but be motivated to push yourself a little harder and give it your all.

If the very thought of boot camp has you shaking in your sneakers, take heart. Not all boot camps are the same, and it may just take some trial and error before you find a class you love. In-your-face instructors aren't for everyone, and if you don't thrive in a tough love environment, you may be a bit intimidated. But I guarantee it is possible to find a high-intensity class that doesn't feel like torture. Also keep in mind that HIIT classes can be adjusted to whatever your personal pace and skill level are, and if you stick with it, you'll continue to improve and get stronger. Oftentimes, completing the first class is all it takes to get hooked. Once you finish that first class, you might emerge drenched in sweat and tired, but your confidence will be through the roof. And there's seriously nothing better than feeling like you just completed a badass boot camp and challenged your body and mind to toughen up. Not into classes? No problem. HIIT workouts can be done solo also. See page 122 for options.

Here are some celebrities who love boot camp:

- Kim Kardashian
- Katie Holmes
- Kelly Ripa
- Carrie Underwood

Workout #3: Yoga

Ancient traditions have a funny way of becoming
major fads, and there's really nothing more seriously
trending than the ancient Indian practice of yoga. But
trust me when I say there's so much more to this
mind-body-spirit practice than Instagrammable poses
and postures. I love yoga because you can practice it
anywhere, without any equipment. I like going to
classes at studios, but I also do DVDs and even
YouTube videos if I am traveling or just don't have
time to leave the house.

In Indian scriptures, yoga is described as a journey
of the self through the self and to the self. More so
than any other workout (because it's so much more
than a workout), yoga focuses on the importance of
recognizing the multifaceted nature of the human
body and spirit, and it works to create a union of your
mind, body, and breath. The goal of yoga is to bring
about health and well-being physically, emotionally,

and mentally through a regular practice of postures (or **asanas**) and breathing techniques. Yoga also focuses on relaxation and concentration at different points throughout the practice. All of this mental work teaches you to focus inward and create a flow of energy through your body and a stream of consciousness that's isolated from all the super-distracting stimuli in your surroundings and in your life.

There are many different branches of yoga, but **hatha yoga** is the type most commonly practiced in exercise or fitness settings. The combinations of asanas are designed to help increase strength while stimulating various *chakras* within the body. The Sanskrit word *chakra* means "wheel" or "disk," and it's used to describe "wheels" of energy in the body, which are thought to correspond to specific nerve centers. When a specific chakra is targeted through an asana, it helps to strengthen and purify your body while helping you gain awareness and control.

If the chakra philosophy is not your cup of tea, you can't deny the fact that yoga increases flexibility, opens up your joints, and seriously stretches your muscles, all while emphasizing positive energy and thinking. (Who doesn't need more of that?)

Yoga also connects you with your breath, which is a critical piece in the energy cycle. If you constantly feel sluggish and lethargic, there's a good chance you're not breathing in a way that's infusing your body with oxygen; yoga can fix that. A regular yoga practice can help you with relaxation, improve your core strength, build strong leg muscles, and get your arms in super-fierce shape. And guess what? If mindless snacking is a problem you can't seem to nip in the bud, yoga might be the answer. You'll become so much more aware of your feelings and in turn become reacquainted with your long-lost hunger/fullness cues.

Now here's the part where all the nonbelievers roll their eyes and say, "But yoga isn't a good workout!" Um, wrong! Maybe you haven't found a class that really challenges you, but some of the best bodies are created through yoga. In fact, those statuesque physiques you see stomping the Victoria's Secret fashion show runway are known to be total yoginis. Models like Gigi Hadid say yoga has helped their bodies become leaner and stronger. And I don't know about you, but I'll totally take a body like Gigi's.

Celebrities who love yoga include:

- Jennifer Aniston
- Gwyneth Paltrow
- Gisele Bündchen
- Jessica Biel

Shaking It Up: The Science Behind Changing Up Your Workout

Okay, so you've finally found a workout you love. Congrats! Now do something totally different. Say what?!

Adding variety to your workouts helps you avoid a plateau, and it also increases your body's ability to efficiently and effectively burn calories. Additionally, one little-known fact of mixing it up is that doing the same type of workout can create **repetitive strain injuries**. These are injuries that happen when you are constantly doing a lot of the same movements (think boxing, weight lifting, or even running). Varying your workouts will give your joints and muscles a break and will let you properly recover and recuperate so you don't end up couch-bound with a sprain or other issue.

The first question people ask when I tell them to mix it up is: How much exercise am I supposed to be doing, exactly?! You know I always keep it real, so while I'd love to tell you that just 10 to 15 minutes a day will get you Kate Hudson abs, but that's not the truth. To receive the maximum physical and mental benefit from exercise, you need to work out most days of the week (that means 4 or 5) for at least 30 to 45 minutes each time.

If you don't believe me, here's the science behind why exercise needs to be a part of your daily routine as much as brushing your teeth or answering nature's call. A University of California, San Francisco study from 2010 showed that stressed-out women who exercised vigorously for about 45 minutes had cells that showed fewer signs of aging compared to women who were stressed and inactive.[33] Another study from the University of Arizona also showed that regular exercise could reduce your risk of developing osteoporosis.[34] Strengthening exercises like hiking, climbing, and weightlifting can keep your bones strong and healthy and protect you from falls, particularly as you age.

Now before you freak out and start pointing to all your meeting notifications, doctor's appointments, and Facebook event invites, trust me, I get it. We all lead busy lives, and sometimes workouts get cut short. So while you *should* strive for consistent, 30- to 45-minute sessions almost every day, the main thing I want you to know is that *any* amount of exercise is better than none. That's because there are *so* many benefits that you don't want to entirely cheat yourself of. For example, did you know exercise can also help you become more coordinated and improve your balance? So if you're kind of clumsy like I am, you can actually avoid taking a nasty spill more than once a week (as I often do).

Still not convinced? The Harvard School of Public Health noted that just 20 minutes of regular exercise improves sexual response in women.[35] Um, pretty awesome, no? And exercise can also remedy constipation and improve your skin because it enhances blood flow. Plus, that strong, sexy feeling you get after a workout will increase your motivation to stay on track with healthy eating.

Look, we're all short on time. But even if you can't fit in an hour-long sweat session, you can still commit to a fitness routine that works for your lifestyle. Don't believe me? It may not be as effective as a HIIT session, but 15 minutes of walking on an incline while scrolling through Instagram still counts. And so do those squats you squeeze in during your shower. Piecing together 10-minute sessions multiple times throughout the day can get your workout done without skipping a beat, and don't forget you can always split your exercise into 15-minute mini sessions in the morning and evening.

Personally, I find a pre-workday workout class to be especially beneficial. The best part of working out in the a.m. is that you have to get ready only once for the day and then you free up time later on in the evening. Another added benefit of exercising early is that it helps you stay on a healthier path all day. When you work out first thing in the morning, your body continues to burn calories throughout the day, and I guarantee you'll think twice before reaching for the Cinnabon. When you think back to your hard work in the early hours, you'll remember just how difficult it actually is to burn 100 calories.

Another big excuse I hear from non-exercisers is the simple fact that group fitness classes and gym memberships cost hard-earned cash. Not everyone is excited to invest their earnings into access to the fancy Equinox locker room or unlimited SoulCycle rides. But putting aside all the hype and all the celebrity endorsements for a second, remember that your workouts are for you. If you can't afford memberships and classes, or you just don't want to spend your money on them, that's okay. Workouts don't have to be expensive. Take a few moments to research classes around you because oftentimes, you can get a discount on a pack of classes or get the first class free. This also allows you to change up your workout while trying something new. If cost is still a concern, you can look into purchasing a DVD series or use YouTube to do specific free workouts.

STAYING ACTIVE WHILE RECOVERING FROM AN INJURY

We've covered what to do when you're bored and broke, but what if you're broken? If you're going to be active, you have to accept the fact that you might sustain an injury. Injuries are common from exercise or even from day-to-day activities. Whether you tripped at the office wearing high heels or you rolled your ankle rushing your toddler out the door, you can sustain an injury that jams up your workout mojo.

Even with an injury, workouts can be done with very low impact, such as Pilates or even walking. The key is to keep moving in some way, even with an injury. Research has also shown that people who've sustained back injuries tend to do better when they are physically active as opposed to staying in bed.

If you have a lower back injury or hip pain, try to move gently but frequently. Light walking or stretching with a foam roller can be a valuable way to help your body bounce back to baseline in no time.

It may feel like a setback, but try to remember that even a minor injury can often be a helpful way to refocus and devote some energy to other areas of your body that may need strengthening and extra attention.

If you do have the funds to invest, but simply don't think it's worth it, studies show that when people have a financial investment associated with exercise, they are more likely to show up and push themselves more.

If you've got $20 on the line, you'll probably make an appearance at that 6 p.m. yoga class. But if you wait for 6 p.m. to roll around before making a decision, you'll probably pop open a beer instead of popping into that Pilates class. If, however, you really do think you can self-motivate and squeeze those workouts in without the investment or external motivation, here are my favorite at-home exercise options:

- *Insanity* by BeachBody
- *30-Day Shred* by Jillian Michaels
- *Bikini Body Guide* by Kayla Itsines
- Yoga videos by Steve Ross (available online/ YouTube)

Utilizing a combo of these workouts and keeping in mind the following tips will have you on the path to success in no time.

Tips for Exercising

Stick to these basic rules as often as possible:

Exercise four or five times per week for 30 to 45 minutes. Pull out your calendar. You're going to make a daily exercise date with yourself! Schedule in activity just like you would a meeting.

Avoid doing the same workout on two consecutive

days. Organize your workouts with this in mind. If you go running, avoid doing it again the next day and swap in a different workout instead.

Don't beat yourself up if you miss a day. This is a biggie. Rather than ridicule yourself, the best thing you can do is just pick up your workout the next day. A single day won't derail you, but an entire month will! The most important thing is to consider a missed day a temporary fluke, move on, and just make sure to get your workout in the next day. Don't get down on yourself. (That will just make it easier to fall prey to self-pity and Ben & Jerry's.) Just make sure missing exercise doesn't become a daily habit.

Do not skip the stretching part of classes, yoga sessions, or cooldowns after running. These are crucial for optimal exercise benefits and for mental growth and clarity. Additionally, you can avoid injuries by properly cooling down and lowering your heart rate safely.

Hire a trainer for a couple of sessions. Many gyms offer one free session with a trainer, so take advantage. A trainer can critique and help you improve your form for certain exercises so you can get the maximum benefit and avoid injuries in the future.

Combine exercise with socializing. Exercising with a friend is a great way to catch up and get a great workout in. Personally, I like to work out solo because it's my favorite kind of "me" time, but if I'm long overdue for a girlfriend catch-up, I often propose getting together for a workout and grabbing a healthy shake or snack afterward. This is an easy way to connect without a huge calorie fest or gossip session. Ain't nobody got time for that!

Don't compare yourself to others. The key to becoming leaner and cleaner is following your journey. When you compare yourself to others, you see only their results, not the path they took to get there. Each person has her own physical and mental goals and struggles. Focus on using others as positive motivation or aspiration, not as another tool for self-criticism.

Use social media positively. Even celebs scour Instagram for body inspiration, and you can too! If there is a particular workout or trend you want to try, find a blogger or Instagram community that is doing this program. You can connect with others, and chances are you will stick with the plan. Bikini Body Guide by Kayla Itsines is a great example of this.

Exercise Summary

- Exercise is a **must**, not just for the physical benefits but working out can immediately boost your mood.
- The best exercise is the one you will actually do.
- The three types of exercises I personally love are the Megaformer, HIIT (high intensity interval training), and yoga.
- Workouts don't have to be expensive. You can get free videos on YouTube or Instagram.
- Change up your workout so you can avoid injury and boredom.
- Exercising for at least 30 minutes daily will get you the maximum benefit, but you can break this up if you don't have 30 minutes all at once.

Here is my favorite exercise playlist:
- "Touch the Sky"—Kanye West
- "Under Control"—Calvin Harris
- "Greenlight"—Pitbull
- "Unforgettable"—French Montana
- "Sugar"—Maroon 5
- "The Mack"—Nevada, Mark
- "Flashback"—Calvin Harris
- "You're the Best" (From Karate Kid)—Joe "Bean" Esposito

Here are my favorite cool down songs:
- "Is This Love"—Bob Marley
- "August Day Song"—Bebel Gilberto
- "Vivo Per Lei"—Andrea Bocelli

Sleep

I t's hard to know if the phrase "beauty sleep" really originated from a fairy-tale princess, but there's one thing I know for sure: A night of missed shut-eye leaves me looking *rough*. The truth about beauty sleep goes well beyond your outer beauty, however. A good night's rest is a fundamental cornerstone of helping you build a lean, clean, and beautiful you on the inside and out.

Ever skimped on sleep and then spent the day chugging caffeinated mochas and inhaling junk food to keep your energy up? That's no coincidence. People who are chronically sleep deprived or get less than five hours of sleep on a regular basis are more likely to pig out on high-calorie and high-sugar snacks. One study found that women who have limited sleep are more likely to gain weight.[36]

As sleep deprivation worsens and accumulates over time, your body increases its production of cortisol, the stress hormone. Guess what that does? If you answered, "It makes me a cravings-crazed monster," you're right! That sleepy, stressed state will lead you to reach for any and all carbs and sugars to get an instant energy boost. That's why one of the most talked-about ways celebrities lose weight and keep it off is by getting adequate sleep. Seriously! If you're a celebrity interview connoisseur like I am, you'll notice many of Hollywood's elite say they'll compromise a workout if it means they can log a few more hours of sleep, especially in the days leading up to red carpet events. Catching more z's helps them feel rested, making it easier to resist temptation and maintain a lower weight than if they were to chug Red Bull all day and night to exercise at the expense of sleep.

How much sleep do you really need? Most experts agree that adults need about **seven to nine hours** of sleep each night to function optimally. Why so much? Well, there's a whole lot going on during a single night's rest. In a normal sleep cycle, you close your eyes, drift off, and your brain releases a hormone called **melatonin**. Your core temperature and your heart rate drop to prepare for this restorative period, and as you move toward sleep, other hormones in your body start to work their magic too.

There are a couple of different stages of sleep, and

they're all super important in their own ways. During a stage called **slow-wave sleep**, hormones are released to help your body and mind heal, repair, and recuperate. This is considered the most restorative and refreshing sleep, and it's when many metabolic processes, particularly hormone balancing and tissue repair, occur.

During **rapid eye movement (REM)** sleep, on the other hand, your brain focuses on forming memories and evaluating all the information you've picked up in the past 24 hours. Unlike slow-wave sleep, REM sleep occurs in short bursts throughout the night. When it happens, your body temperature and heart rate rise.

Your body needs both sleep phases to function adequately and to help keep your cells healthy and avoid damage. Without the right amount of sleep, you put your body at an increased risk for infection, weight gain, and mental fog.

But if you're chronically stressed or super anxious, your brain might be on drill sergeant mode, sending out work orders all day and night. This (unsurprisingly) impairs your ability to wind down and fall asleep and impedes the time it takes to get to slow-wave sleep. When you're sleep deprived, your body starts to have an abnormal response to insulin. And you already know how that can impact your health and weight. (Hint: It ain't good.)

Okay, but I Feel Great after Two Hours of Sleep a Night

Still not convinced that sleep is powerful medicine? Consider one study done by researchers at the University of Pennsylvania and Washington State University.[37] At the beginning of the experiment, a group of healthy men and women who were averaging about seven hours of sleep per night were split into different groups. The first group slept four hours per night, the second group slept six hours per night, and the third group slept eight hours per night.

Surprise: Subjects who slept for eight hours didn't have any cognitive deficits, problems with attention, or difficulty with motor skills. Lucky them. The other groups? Not so fortunate. The group that slept only four hours was by far the worst at cognitive tasks and performance, and the group that slept six hours wasn't all that much more impressive. The study found that after one week, 25 percent of the people who slept only six hours were falling asleep at random times throughout the day. People in the six-hour group who sustained this schedule for two weeks straight also made lots of mistakes during the day. And these weren't minor boo-boos: They were errors that researchers considered just as significant as if the participants had stayed up for 48 hours straight.

Unfortunately, women have to hold themselves to a higher standard when it comes to sleep compared with men. Edward Suarez, PhD, professor of psychiatry at Duke University, found that sleep-deprived females have higher levels of stress, anxiety, and mood swings compared to equally sleep-deprived males.[38] This is thought to be in part because males produce more testosterone, which counteracts stress hormones like cortisol. Ugh, unfair, I know. Consider that one more reason why sleep is such an essential part of being a fully functioning, do-it-all super-woman.

What to Do When Counting Sheep Doesn't Cut It

If you're not sure how to get enough z's, I've got plenty of tips that can help improve your sleep, ensuring it's the most powerful weapon possible to aid in your mission to become leaner and cleaner. Take a look:

Avoid caffeine. Many of us can agree, coffee is amazing. But eliminating caffeine after the early a.m. hours can be an easy way to help your body reset its natural sleep pattern. It's especially important to refrain from using caffeine as a pick-me-up in the afternoon.

Set the right temperature. Believe it or not, the best temperature to fall asleep comfortably is around 70 degrees. (It's also the safest sleeping temperature for newborns and young children.) If your thermostat is set to tropical conditions, take it down a notch.

Use white noise if you're a light sleeper. If every creak and cough wakes you up, consider dropping $20 (or less) on a white noise machine specifically designed to camouflage distracting sounds.

Keep it consistent. It's super important to start dozing off and waking up around the same times each day to train your body to get great-quality sleep. When you stick to a sleep schedule, your body learns to find a true rhythm and properly secrete hormones to help you regulate your own sleep-wake cycle.

Black out the room. Everyone loves a well-lit living space, but keep your bedroom cave-like when you're snoozing. Even the slightest light stimulation can keep you up or wake you up way too soon. If your bedroom isn't dark enough, use blackout shades or sleep with an eye mask to help you achieve complete darkness, which can help lull you to sleep more quickly as well as help you stay asleep.

Keep work at work. Your bedroom is for sleep

and sexy time. That's it. So avoid bringing your office to-do list anywhere near this sacred space. When you use your bedroom to do work or cognitive tasks, your brain gets reactivated, making it much more difficult to get to sleep. This is the reason I also discourage my patients from getting cozy under the covers with their laptops to catch up on emails or max out their credit cards with online shopping. Use your bed as a restorative and relaxing space only. When you keep all work-related stuff elsewhere, your brain will pick up on the fact that the bed is solely for purposes that require little analytical thinking.

Avoid alcohol and food too close to bedtime. Boozing or eating a meal right before bed can be a disaster for good sleep. When food enters your stomach, your body focuses all its attention on utilizing and storing the energy load. It also releases insulin to manage the intake instead of powering down for sleep. And sorry to be the bearer of bad news, but it's true: Research has shown that chowing down too close to bedtime may actually lead to weight gain.[44]

Try a supplement. If you've tried everything and still can't sleep, melatonin is a great option for inducing slumber. Try three to five milligrams, one hour before bedtime. You can also try a supplement called **L-theanine** if you are having trouble relaxing or anxiety is getting in the way of your sleep. It's an amino acid that's been shown to increase levels of feel-good, relaxing hormones.

Exercise. Yet another reason I always advocate for exercise: It helps you sleep! Working out helps you get to sleep faster and stay asleep longer. Exercising early in the day helps reduce cortisol levels for up to 12 hours and can have a positive impact on a good night's sleep. Researchers have also shown that people who engage in at least 30 minutes of moderate cardio in the morning tend to fall asleep quicker and stay asleep for more hours.[45] These people also spend up to 75 percent more time in deep sleep than people who work out later in the day.

Breathe, unplug, and clear your mind. Whether you have a formal meditation practice or the word "meditation" makes you cringe, taking 5 to 10 minutes right before bed to close your eyes and focus on taking deep breaths can really help put your body and brain in the right place for rest.

Get a good ritual in place. If you have kids or have ever been around little ones, you know they thrive on routine. But here's a pearl: Most adults do too! Before we tuck kids in, we usually turn off the TV, put away the toys, give them a warm bath, and turn down all the lights. Have you ever seen a kid going crazy on the iPad and bingeing on snacks go straight to sleep with zero struggle? If so, please call me and also trademark your parenting tips immediately! Kids and grown-ups alike need special time before bed so their brains can get the signal that it's time to quiet down. Start establishing your own sleep routine. Warm baths are acceptable at any age.

My Brain Doesn't Turn Off!

Is it just me, or does bedtime seem like the exact hour your brain decides it's time to go into overdrive to compose grocery lists, obsess over work emails, or replay awkward social interactions from the previous 10 years? Anxiety and worry are surefire stimulants that can keep you wide-eyed at night. One thing I've found to be super helpful in dealing with this incessant brain dialogue is to get my thoughts down on paper—like, actual, literal paper, not the digital kind. Instead of trying to compile a mental list or jot down your thoughts on a bright device, the best way to clear your mind is to keep a good, old-fashioned pen and paper right next to your bed so you can quickly and easily thought dump as necessary. Once you actually write down the ideas bouncing around in your head, it becomes much easier to compartmentalize and fall asleep.

(continued on page 138)

THE AFTERNOON SLUMP

You're sitting at your desk post-lunch, staring at your screen when you realize just how comfortable your chair is and how nice it would feel to rest your eyes for a minute or two. Before you know it, you're fantasizing about your comfy bed and can't believe you still have three more hours at the office. Welcome to your afternoon slump.

If this scenario sounds way too familiar, you're in good company; most of us start to feel a little (or a lot) slower midday. But before you write it off as laziness, listen up: There are biological reasons for this lull in energy. Your **hypothalamus**, the portion of your brain responsible for everything from hunger and heart rate to blood pressure and body temperature—and yes, sleep—likes to keep a strict schedule. Your **circadian rhythm** (the 24-hour sleep/wake cycle) is pre-programmed to have peaks and valleys through the day. According to the National Sleep Foundation, one of those major valleys happens to fall approximately between 1 and 3 p.m.[39] One potential reason for that drowsiness may have to do with a natural dip in your core temperature, which signals your brain and body to get sleepy. This happens around bedtime, and experts say a mini-dip also happens during that afternoon window.

Unfortunately, only a select few cultures incorporate afternoon siestas into the workday. The rest of us, who must power through, have to rely on some tried-and-true methods for staving off sleepiness. Luckily, there are plenty of ways to stay awake and alert, and they don't involve venti triple-shot caffeine concoctions.

Take a quick lap around the block. It doesn't take much

exercise to get a big energy boost. One study found that a brisk 10-minute walk improved energy and lowered tension.[40]

Skip the sugar. The same study found that a sugary snack was associated with an initial jolt of energy, which was quickly followed by a crash. It also found that a sugary snack created significantly higher tension after one hour.

Cut the unhealthy fat. An Australian study found that higher fat consumption was associated with increased daytime sleepiness,[41] and another study published in the journal *SLEEP* found similar results.[42] While healthy fats like avocado and coconut oil can help keep you full and satisfied, too much fat is never good, especially from foods like greasy burgers.

Balance is your friend. Overeating can lead to a food coma, but undereating will leave you feeling depleted. Rather than having an all-or-nothing mentality around lunchtime, go for balance, incorporating a healthy mix of fat, carbs, and protein to keep your blood sugar stable and your energy consistent.

Drink up. Dehydration can definitely leave you feeling limp and listless, so make sure you're sipping enough H_2O throughout the day. Don't wait until you're parched to fill your glass.

See the light. Research has shown that exposure to natural light can help decrease afternoon sleepiness. If you can't go out for a walk, at least park your laptop near a window.[43]

Get enough sleep! This should go without saying, but you can't expect to take on the day without the proper rest at night. Remember that you have an internal body clock that doesn't shift according to your late-night work load. Most adults need seven to nine hours of sleep a night. If you're not getting that, it's time to rethink your nighttime routine.

If the writing tactic doesn't do the trick, then it's time to use technology for good. Even though electronics are generally a big no-no in the bedroom, they can be a great tool if you use them correctly. For example, tons of sleep apps can actually track how much shut-eye you're getting, and they can be programmed to wake you up at just the right time.

If you've ever felt super tired during the day despite logging the right amount of hours of sleep, it could be because your alarm started sounding in the middle of a deep stage of sleep. Certain apps can help wake you more naturally than a blaring alarm that jars you into consciousness. They can be programmed to sound only during lighter stages of sleep within 10 to 15 minutes of your set wake-up time.

Try the following apps:

- HeadSpace
- Sleep Cycle
- Calm

Sleep Summary

- Everybody needs sleep. We need it for critical cell functioning, to repair our muscles, and to relax our mind.

- Poor sleep is associated with a host of medical conditions, including obesity, uncontrolled diabetes, and anxiety.

- Set the right environment to make your sleep successful. This includes avoiding electronics, keeping your room cool, not bringing work to bed, and exercising earlier in the day.

- Anxiety and/or an overloaded schedule can lead to poor sleep or difficulty getting to sleep. Write down your concerns or list of to-dos on actual paper instead of worrying and letting thoughts circle in your head.

- Afternoon sleepiness can be a problem. Keep your blood sugar in balance to avoid falling asleep at your desk.

- Consider using sleep apps to track and improve your sleep.

5

Supplements

Less fat, more energy, shrink cellulite, boost brainpower. I've seen it all on hundreds of bottles, and you probably have too. You might have even waltzed down a store aisle thinking you got your hands on the hottest weight loss trend of the season. Around $39 to $80 later you probably realized the answer isn't in a bottle, and now you've got an expensive paper weight.

The supplement industry is expansive and confusing. But don't worry, I've got your cheat sheet right here so you can navigate your way through supplement city with ease.

Why Supplement?

Supplements are just what their name indicates: They're meant to be *supplemental*. The bottom line is that nothing replaces a healthy and well-rounded diet. But getting a little help from supplements can provide the extra oomph your day-to-day intake may be lacking.

My patients often come to me with questions about supplements because they heard a celebrity raving about a particular type of pill or potion.

One famous name that comes up frequently is Suzanne Somers. I *love* Suzanne. In fact, I grew up watching *Three's Company*, and all these years later, I can still hear her character Chrissy snort-laughing her way out of hilarious hijinks. Since her TV heyday, however, Somers has become better known for publicly touting the benefits of taking almost 40 supplements per day.

Even as a fangirl, I have to draw the line here. I have yet to meet any patient, friend, or acquaintance who needs that many supplements to thrive. If you're eating a healthy diet, exercising, sleeping, and keeping your stress in check, a little should go a long way when it comes to supplements.

Choosing which supplements to use, however, can feel like a major guessing game. If you've ever walked into Whole Foods on the hunt for a probiotic, you've come face-to-face with more than 20 choices. With so many brands, formulations, and eye-catching marketing claims, it's understandable why so many people have tons of questions when it comes to finding the right supplement.

First of all, it's important to know that while federal law requires dietary supplements to be labeled as such, there's no law requiring these products to be proven safe according to the FDA's standards. In fact, supplement manufacturers don't have to prove that the claims they make are honest or accurate. Once a supplement is on the market, the FDA monitors certain safety regulations, but manufacturers don't have to get any kind of stamp of approval to produce or sell their products. Kinda scary, right?

The good news is that while some brands are considered higher quality than others, you don't have to spend a fortune to find the right fit. The most important thing is to pay attention to some overarching shopping guidelines and choose a product that fits your life and budget while providing the desired effects. Here are some tips:

Be wary of over-the-top claims. If the claims on the bottle or package sound too good to be true, they likely are. There's no magic pill that will "melt fat" or "cure" anything. (Trust me, it would've been on *Shark Tank* by now.) Before you even consider taking a supplement, no matter the brand, check in with your doctor and talk about the potential risks and benefits.

Think critically about news headlines. If you run out and buy every supplement you read about in the news, you'll likely wind up with a jam-packed medicine cabinet and a whole lot of disappointment. New research is coming out all the time on supplements, but scientific discoveries are small and subtle. While the media loves to turn every minor observation into front-page news, it's important to understand the context of the studies and if/how the particular research applies to you and your health.

"Natural" doesn't equal "safe." This is a big one. Many of us have learned to associate marketing terms like "natural," "wholesome," "organic," and even "gluten-free" with products that are safe and/or effective. But plenty of "natural" ingredients can be toxic or have adverse reactions when combined with certain medications. That's why it's more important for you to know your particular health situation than to follow product labels or advertising claims.

Know what the certifications mean. The FDA requires supplements to follow **"good manufacturing practices,"** or **GMPs**. Some manufacturers pay an extra fee to prove to consumers they've been tested and approved by independent organizations. These groups have an added layer of testing and can provide you with more detailed information. These include the following.

- **ConsumerLab.com** is a private company that randomly buys and analyzes popular supplements. They test ingredients, strength, whether the product is contaminated, and whether it disintegrates.

- **NSF International** is a nonprofit that evaluates bottled water and filters as well as supplements. This organization tests products to make sure their ingredient labels are accurate and they don't contain contaminants.

- **The U.S. Pharmacopeia Convention (USP)** is a nonprofit that sets standards for drug manufacturers and has a Dietary Supplement Verification Program. It doesn't just test the final product. It conducts on-site audits of manufacturing plants too.

Avoid products with unnecessary additives and fillers. You shouldn't need tons of sugar or artificial flavors or colors in your supplements, or in anything, really, but they're particularly out of place here. Check the label on your supplements before buying.

Do your research. Before buying a supplement, take the time to look for scientific studies online from legitimate journals that back up the claims of the manufacturer. Always investigate the brand's website. It's a good sign when a brand is transparent about the resources and funding that go into research and development.

Aim for midrange products. Some supplements will seem astronomically expensive, while others will seem suspiciously low-cost. If you're not sure if the product is worth the investment or if you should try to save, it's a good idea to do some comparison shopping and keep your selection to the mid-cost options.

The Supplements You Actually Need

While less is more, there are certain supplements I think everyone could benefit from. Here are the ones your body will thank you for.

Omega-3s

Remember omega-3s from Chapter 1? They're the group of fatty acid compounds with anti-inflammatory properties. Two of the most important fatty acids are DHA and EPA. Supplements should have at least 600 to 1,000 milligrams of both DHA and EPA. Omega-3s are known as essential fatty acids, meaning your body needs them but can't create them on its own. That's why you have to get them from food or supplements. The daily recommendation for omega-3s is one gram total of EPA and DHA. You may recall that ALA is a vegetarian/plant-based source of omega-3s found in foods like walnuts, vegetable oils, and flaxseeds, while DHA and EPA are primarily found in fish oil.

Remember why we need omega-3s? They've been shown to decrease inflammation, promote cell repair, and preserve cellular integrity, particularly in the skin. There's also good data to suggest they have a positive impact on cholesterol levels.

Because omega-3s primarily come from fish oil, it's important to find a supplement that's safe and healthy. That means the supplement you choose should be free of synthetic chemicals and mercury. Many omega-3 supplements contain tocopherol a.k.a. vitamin E to protect the integrity of the DHA and EPA and prevent spoilage, so don't shy away from a brand that includes these additions too.

Probiotics

Popping a probiotic is crucial. Probiotics are healthy bacteria that can help protect and rebuild your gut. They also help protect against a weakened immune system and have been found to be super helpful in restoring healthy bowel function to people who struggle with problems in the bathroom. Most probiotics contain **lactobacillus** and **bifidobacterium**.

These are types of microorganisms that help maintain a healthy balance of good bacteria in your GI tract to preserve the integrity of your digestive system—no easy feat.

Within your GI tract, you may have 500 or more different types of bacterial species. In 2010, a large *Cochrane* review showed that people who took probiotics while dealing with a GI illness were sick for an average of 25 hours *less* than those who didn't take probiotics, and there was a significant reduction in diarrhea and length of time that diarrhea lasted.[44] If you've ever spent a night running to the bathroom, then you can appreciate what wonderful news this is.

Probiotics also made headlines when a Stanford University study found that obese people have different gastrointestinal bacteria than normal-weight people. This was a breakthrough finding that really illustrated how GI bacterial content plays a hugely influential role in our weight.

Another study of postpartum women who were trying to lose abdominal fat showed that adding lactobacillus and bifidobacterium capsules helped reduce their waist circumference. A UCLA study noted that regular consumption of a probiotic-containing yogurt improved brain function,[45] and researchers found that consumption of yogurt may actually change the way your brain responds to the environment. Finally, researchers have noted how bacteria found in the gut can affect the way the body metabolizes sugars and glucose, so popping a probiotic is a crucial way to keep on top of your health.

B Complex

B vitamins play an important role in all kinds of cellular processes within your body, and taking a B complex will help you get a bunch of these guys in one fell swoop. Without these vitamins, your immune system wouldn't be able to do its incredibly important job, so they're a big deal. Here's what they do: B_1 is needed during the process of carbohydrate breakdown, and B_2 (or **riboflavin**) is necessary to help fight cellular damage in the body and has also been thought to help with the aging process. B_6 is known to help sleep and mood, and B_7 (or **biotin**) helps boost hair and nail growth.

Vitamin D

Vitamin D assists in the development of strong bones and teeth. It's also known that people with many other medical illnesses such as depression, elevated blood pressure, and chronic fatigue often happen to be deficient in vitamin D. Although you can get vitamin D from foods and sunlight, it's extremely common to be deficient, so I recommend 1,000 IU daily to my patients. If your doctor diagnoses you with a deficiency, however, you may need more.

Added Fiber Supplements

Glucomannan powder comes from the Asian **konjac plant**. It's a soluble fiber that helps bulk the stool and promotes satiety. The greater the stickiness of fiber, the more efficient it is at eliminating waste and promoting a feeling of fullness. Some studies have also shown that when combined with exercise, glucomannan powder helps reduce bloating and total body fat, and it also improves cholesterol numbers and feelings of fullness.

Glucomannan becomes a gel/paste-like substance that forms a layer around food and limits the absorption of highly caloric foods. This powder also absorbs water very quickly, which triggers intestinal movement. All around, it's a worthy supplement to incorporate into your regimen if you're struggling with constipation.

Psyllium powder. This is a type of bulking fiber that increases your stool quantity and also draws water into the stool to help make stool passage easier and less painful. Psyllium comes from the seeds of a plant and is used as a natural bulking agent and found in many "fiber fortified" cereals and flours. Products like Metamucil also contains psyllium, but have artificial sweeteners and dyes. Naturally occurring psyllium husk powder is a great source of added fiber. You can add a small amount to your water bottle or even mix into yogurt or hummus.

No one likes to talk about it, but one of the most overlooked reasons why people feel sluggish and can't seem to truly master a leaner, cleaner lifestyle is a poorly functioning digestive system. Your gut is responsible for a big part of your overall health. Some cultures even consider the gastrointestinal (GI) system to be the second brain of the body. If you look at ancient Ayurvedic and Eastern medicine practices focusing on the GI system, they note that hormone absorption and the health of your gut lining can be the key to achieving and maintaining overall well-being and a healthy weight.

Check any embarrassment at the door because we're about to get specific. Many people define **constipation** as a sense of feeling backed up and the inability to use the bathroom regularly. But what does "regular" even mean? Well, if you're only emptying your bowels as often as your *Entertainment Weekly* shows up in your

HOW TO COMBAT CONSTIPATION

If you're constipated, there are several medically proven ways to help get your gut moving again.

- **Drink plenty of water and fluids.** You already know this is a big part of getting your body leaner and cleaner. Lack of fluid is one of the primary reasons for chronic constipation. The fluid helps make stool soft and malleable, helping it move more easily through the intestines and colon, and into the bowl. That may sound gross, but not as gross as being full of sh!% (literally).

- **Try yoga poses.** Work with a yoga instructor or do some quick Googling to tackle these poses: **wind-relieving pose** (yes, that's really the name), **sitting spinal twist**, and **half plow**. All of these poses are designed to create movement and flow and relieve pressure within the GI tract. They can help stimulate areas of the colon and relieve pressure or pockets of air that may be contributing to chronic backup. Practice each move in a series 5 to 10 times and hold for 15 to 20 seconds each.

- **Supplement your stool.** Using a fiber supplement will help bulk your stool and get your colon on track to emptying regularly and efficiently.

- **Drink hot water and lemon.** Drinking two cups of hot water with lemon every morning can also help get your gut going.

The exception: If you're having very thin, stringy, or mucousy stool or if you notice any blood in your bowel movements, you should see your physician to determine the cause before continuing any type of program. This can be a sign of something more serious that needs to be evaluated.

mailbox, that's not enough. Sure, this may be a "regular" schedule, but it's not a safe one. Your body was designed to eliminate waste after every meal. Yes, seriously! As you learned earlier, the two types of fiber—soluble and insoluble—help bulk up your stool and keep your gastrointestinal receptors in check, allowing for you to empty your bowels more frequently and have smooth bowels movements that don't cause trouble or straining.

The symptoms of an out-of-whack gut can show up in all kinds of places. Here are a few indications your gut health is in need of an overhaul:

- Increasing acne
- Frequent gas and bloating
- Feeling very tired or having a depressed mood
- Bad breath despite regular flossing and brushing

The GI tract is one of the few but mighty ways of eliminating toxins from the body. Often without knowing it, we ingest toxins from our environment. Most often, our bodies process these toxins and send them out through the gut. All of those unintentionally ingested chemicals, pesticides, hormones, and other impurities need an exit strategy, and without regular stool elimination, you absorb these waste products. This can lead to constipation and reabsorption of toxins.

Some studies also suggest that chronic constipation

can alter the lining of your intestines, making you more likely to reabsorb particles that should be excreted. All of this ultimately contributes to inflammation and obesity, which are two issues you don't want to invite into your life.

Multivitamins

Sometimes patients want to know, "Can't I just take an all in one multivitamin?" Maybe. The benefit of a multivitamin is the convenience of taking only one pill.

The drawbacks, however, include not getting enough of the specific vitamins you may need or not knowing the quality or type of each specific vitamin you are looking for.

Additionally, multivitamins can sometimes contain things you don't want like 3000 percent of selenium. If you absolutely must use a multivitamin, take time to research one without any added fillers, unnecessary dyes or ingredients, and that doesn't give you 5000 percent of anything. Otherwise, I suggest sticking to the basics of only what you need (as I mentioned above).

Supplements Summary

- Supplements can be helpful, but they don't replace a healthy diet, they simply supplement it.
- Know what you are buying. Anything that seems too good to be true probably is.
- The supplements that you should consider adding to your daily routine include omega-3s, probiotics, B complex, and vitamin D.
- Fiber supplements can be helpful if you suffer from constipation. Glucomannan powder or psyllium are both good options.
- Multivitamins are not my go-to recommendation because they often contains less of what you want and more of what you don't. If you must take a multi, look for one with only 100 percent of your daily values instead of 500 percent.

Mental Health
and
Mindfulness

I did my first half-marathon with my husband, and although we trained by running almost 11 miles, I was pretty scared of the actual race day and worried about how I would make it those last few miles. The week before the race I asked him how he is always able to push himself, and he said, "It's usually just in your head. If you think you can do it and don't let it get to you, you can usually do it. It isn't really about the physical at that point."

Of course, I figured that was just a husband kind of answer (I know you have heard some of these), so I asked my brother, a triathlete and marathoner, and he said, "Yeah it's just mind over matter." So I guess it was unanimous, and truthfully they were right. The way you think and your outlook on certain situations can make or break your day, week, and life. (Not to be dramatic, but I do believe this!)

Why Mental Health Matters

I know you're eager to get to the plan already, and here I am blabbering about happiness. But hear me out, mental health matters. But why when we're talking about a body transformation? In many ways, mental health is the most important part of The 10-Day Total Body Transformation and this entire book.

Studies have shown that the mental component to your general health, and particularly for weight loss, is as important as the physical component. A positive outlook goes a long way in your overall health and success. Your beliefs and attitudes about your health can make or break your well-intentioned behaviors. By eliminating negativity in your thinking and training your mind to think differently, you'll be able to visualize, achieve, and sustain the results you want—for good.

One *Cochrane* study showed that weight loss programs that evaluate mental health are more success-ful than traditional programs.[46] Researchers have also noted that weight loss and developing a healthy lifestyle are directly correlated with how people handle stress and other negative emotions in their lives. Frequent anxiety and sadness can trigger chemical processes that steer us toward unhealthy and toxic food choices. By breaking free from the cycle of stress and negativity, you're likely to foster change within yourself. When you're constantly in high-stress situations, your body continues to release that notorious stress hormone, cortisol. To maintain this ongoing sense of high alertness, your body will drive you to look for energy through quick sources (sugars, sweets, soda, etc.). But this constant search for satisfaction is not inevitable. You just have to know how to master your mind.

Reclaiming Your Happiness

Think back to the last time you felt happy. Understanding real happiness can be challenging, especially given the obstacles and realities of modern life. Was it when you received a gift from a friend or when you sipped some soothing tea? Or are you having a hard time thinking of anything that wasn't a passing laugh at a *Friends* rerun? (Ross in the leather pants gets me every time.) Do you usually derive happiness from your material possessions? Valuing material things isn't always bad. (I get excited when I look at a beautiful bag or good pair of heels, too.) But your possessions shouldn't define you. In some cases, achieving certain milestones and marking those with material items can be a part of happiness, but the truth is, you're unlikely to actually *be* happy if you're spending all your time seeking material things to accomplish this state of satisfaction.

What you define as happiness may change as you go through different stages of life and are faced with different challenges. Remember when you were so stoked to get a flip phone in the early 2000s? (Okay, not all of you will remember this.) Or how pumped you were to get home in time to watch your favorite shows (before DVRs were a thing)? Nowadays, if you don't have the latest iPhone, or the best job, home, or car, you can feel disappointed and totally unfulfilled. What a difference time makes. But in reality, these things have little to do with true happiness.

Many researchers, professors, and even religious figures have dedicated their lives to determining what creates and maintains happiness. It can be difficult, especially in this current era, to feel or understand true happiness without equating it to material things. It's important, however, to understand that happiness is always relative, and you control your own happiness and attitude. To truly understand this feeling we need to examine three concepts that play a pivotal role in happiness. These include self-reflection, contentment, and gratitude.

Self-reflection. Sometimes you feel great, and sometimes you don't. But it can be hard to understand why. Self-reflection helps you understand your strengths, weaknesses, and provide direction for your life. When you ask many people what is important in life, they will often say "being a good person." But being a "good person" requires you to take a critical look at yourself and identify the traits and attributes that define this type of person. Are you treating others how you like to be treated? Are you blaming others for your setbacks? Can you find ways to improve yourself or channel your energy into something productive? Questioning yourself and looking within can help you better understand your true identity and lead you on the path to happiness.

Contentment is the idea of having satisfaction with all that you have in your life, whether it be material possessions, relationships, career achievements, or physical attributes. Contentment is not a feeling, it is a state of mind or an attitude. When you can develop a sense of contentment, you can start to be truly happy. It is important not to mistake contentment for complacency. Let's say you have a job you are happy with and making enough money to pay for your daily expenditures and living comfortably. An attitude of contentment should not keep you from wanting to advance in your career. Contentment helps you appreciate your life, accept where you are on this journey, and release you from the pressure of external influences.

Gratitude is the most important cornerstone to happiness as it ties together contentment and self-reflection. When you are driven by goals and desires, you can often forget to be thankful and grateful for what you already have. Most people do not realize good health, a roof over your head, food to eat, and a warm place to sleep are not guaranteed for all. If you take a moment to focus on gratitude, you will immediately see the things you take for granted.

After a long labor, I had my first baby via C-section. The days following the C-section were tough, partly because I had never had surgery before. The morning after my baby was born, I had a cough, and my ab muscles started killing—so much that I had to lay down from pain. At that moment, I realized how much I take for granted in terms of good health and daily activities. A few weeks later when I was coughing without pain, I reminded myself of how lucky I am to have recovered from surgery.

Practicing all three of these attributes in harmony is the core of happiness. The more you can understand yourself, the more you will start to feel happier and uplifted. Your enthusiasm for life will grow, and you can finally focus on achieving your goals.

Another gratifying way to achieve happiness is to make others happy through kindness, charity, and goodwill. Think of all the causes and organizations that matter to you and how you might be able to play a small part in the success of those missions.

Remember: Happiness isn't one-dimensional. You have to strive to be happy on a physical, emotional, and spiritual level. That means doing a variety of things to satisfy your need for joy on all levels—in other words, focusing on regular exercise, looking to yourself for contentment, and creating your own road map for what you want to achieve in life. If you take a moment to reflect on your life, do you feel enthusiastic about it? Do you feel blessed and content with what you have and where you are going? Or do you constantly question your purpose and look for something better?

When you're happy, you're way more likely to maintain a healthy and happy lifestyle. People who are feeling down or even depressed lack serotonin, the chemical in your brain that's normally responsible for making you feel happiness and contentment. This hormone also controls your ability to make impulsive choices. A University of Utah study showed that impulse control was higher in people with higher levels of serotonin compared to people with low levels. This means that if you're feeling happy, you're more likely to stick to your plan for a healthy lifestyle instead of reverting back to unhealthy food and lifestyle habits.

The decision to strive toward happiness and positivity comes from within. It's up to you to alter your environment to promote and grow these feelings; these aren't thoughts or feelings you can receive from others. You have to achieve your own happiness and work toward your goals each and every day. By identifying negative factors, people, or environments and choosing to eliminate them from your life, you become that much closer to being leaner, cleaner, and happier. The following tips can help you cultivate feel-good vibes and get on your path to happiness.

Surround yourself with positive people. Even if you're naturally a positive thinker, it's important to find others who are always going to help you see the brighter side of things, especially when you're having some down days. These are people you should feel at ease being around. They're your cheerleaders, and your relationships with them should be effortless. If you find yourself questioning a relationship or wondering whether you should spend time with a certain person, focus instead on a person who reliably provides you with support.

Recognize your relationships. Make a list of all

your important relationships. This includes your spouse, partner, children, coworkers, friends, family members, and anyone else with whom you frequently come in contact with in your day-to-day life. Take a few seconds to identify the good traits of each person. Mark anyone who drains you of energy or with whom you don't enjoy spending time. Once you've identified these people, think more closely about your last few interactions. If these situations were stressful or were centered around nonstop complaints, make a note of this. Now you can consciously make an effort to spend more time with others on your list. By doing that, you'll start to occupy your time by engaging in fun activities and relationships that make you feel excited and thankful to be alive. When you dedicate time to people who inspire you to be a better person, you'll naturally limit or eliminate time with anyone who negatively impacts your life. (*Mean Girls* are for movie night, not for real life.)

Engage in work that you truly love. You're probably familiar with the phrases "do what you love" and "live your life to the fullest," and all those other Pinterest-worthy quotes that are splashed across bright backgrounds on social media. ("Live, laugh, love," amirite?) But are you taking these messages to heart? Engaging in work that you love can be the most therapeutic, transformative, and positive experience in your life. A recent Gallup poll showed that the average person spends about 47.5 hours in the office each week.[47] In some cases, that's more time in the office than at home with family. If you don't enjoy your work, consider work that makes you feel happier. Or, take on another project that you can focus your attention on. In 2015, my father was suddenly diagnosed with leukemia. He fought a strong battle, but he passed away only six months later. The grief of losing my dad was, and sometimes still is, extremely hard for me. But I channeled some of this grief into working on this book as my "project," and I feel a true sense of happiness.

Don't worry about what others think. This is a challenging concept, but it can have huge rewards when mastered. Many times, other people's opinions can drive your relationships, activities, and social media interactions, and even impact your behaviors. If you're lying awake at night wondering what another person thinks about you or wasting your days analyzing other people's commentary or opinions of you, you will have trouble moving forward and living your own life. As much as you can, focus inward, and you will learn to avoid being influenced by outside opinions.

Remember, you create your own life and destiny.

If you're always listening to what other people are doing or reading Facebook posts about the great new relationship your friend is in, it can be tempting to just sink back into your chair and feel sorry for yourself about your lukewarm life. Don't! Take responsibility for designing your own awesome life events and enjoying them to their fullest.

Think about your reaction. A lot of things may seem out of your control, and some are. But the way you react to situations is totally, 100 percent within your power. This means that if something unexpected happens to you, your ability to approach the situation with a positive outlook can make a world of difference. Now let's be serious, these changes aren't going to happen overnight. This isn't Dalai Lama training. But if you acknowledge your desire to change and continue to work at this, the results will speak for themselves.

Focus on the great things going on in your life. Instead of focusing on what you don't like about your job, your partner, your home, etc., notice the good things you have in your life, such as family, friends, nature, and good health. These are all important things you may frequently take for granted, and if you actually practice giving thanks for them, it can make a world of difference. Write down the things that you're really grateful for, and take a few moments daily or weekly to look at the things you can appreciate in life. This is a great way to stay positive and focus on your goals and dreams. It's also an easy way to remember how fortunate you are.

Avoid unhealthy people. If you spend time with people who love to eat poorly or frequently indulge in unhealthy habits, it's likely impacting you more than you realize. Minimizing your time with these people is your best bet. This doesn't mean you should ditch your friends who love to gossip or who indulge in cheese, wine, chocolate, and other sweatpants-worthy foods. It just means you should avoid making a habit of always hanging out with the same group if they don't care at all about being healthy. You'll regret it.

Diversify your portfolio. To the point above, having many groups of friends and outlets can help you spend time with a variety of people who have different outlooks and approaches to life. This can open your eyes to different ways of thinking and improve your ability to be more positive, getting to a better and healthier lifestyle more quickly.

Connect with your support system. A prominent CEO and celebrity once told me, "Each week, I try to remind myself of the things that I have going on in my life. Then I share my list with my spouse over lunch or dinner." When you check in with your support system (a spouse, friend, sibling, or personal coach), it reminds you that you have a very full life and a great group of people supporting you. And if you don't feel like you have a support system? Time to create one! Revisit your list of contacts and schedule a meetup with someone you value. You'd be surprised how helpful this can be.

Avoid relationships that are no longer valuable to your life. In some cases, people grow apart without a major catastrophic falling out that leads to the end of a relationship. Not spending time with a friend can sometimes be a source of frustration and unnecessary stress. Let go of friendships or relationships you're unable or unwilling to put time into. If you lament the loss of a good friendship, rekindle it by reaching out. This way, if your friendship takes off again, you'll be happy you made the effort, and if not, you can move on.

Take a cue from your body. Many times, frustration is more prominent when you're tired, irritable, or hungry. By letting these emotions take over, you're more likely to reach for unhealthy food choices, and you're also likely to find and highlight the negatives of a situation instead of refocusing on the things that are going well. Avoid this problem by staying well-nourished and sticking to your exercise plan.

Change your inner voice. We all have an inner

voice, whether we realize it or not. To positively train and use your inner voice, you have to sit alone with your thoughts and analyze the way you talk to yourself. Do you often hear yourself saying, "I didn't have time for that," or "I should have done x"? Or is it usually, "I had a list of 10 things to do, and I've already finished five—yay me!"? Changing your inner voice and self-talk can be a remarkable way to achieve your goals and feel happier. If you start to focus on the things that you've accomplished, it can propel you forward versus getting caught up in negative self-talk.

Practice forgiveness, especially toward yourself. One of the hardest things to master is the act of forgiveness. Many times, it can be difficult to forgive others, and it can be infinitely more difficult to forgive yourself. If you're frequently caught up in what happened yesterday, last week, or even several years ago, or you find yourself lamenting missed opportunities, this can be a major roadblock in your journey to get healthy. Moving on from the past and using it as a learning experience is your best bet to getting a healthier, leaner, and cleaner mind and body. You'll feel a sense of lightness and ease, and you'll also approach each situation with gratitude and grace.

Create a workspace that makes you happy. Notice the place where you spend the most time during your day. This may be your desk at work, a room at home, your dinner table, your kitchen, or even your car. It's difficult to avoid clutter and chaos when you have a busy life, but taking a few moments to make your workspace welcoming and clean can be a surprisingly refreshing and productive change to your life. Even if many places in your home are chaotic, a calm workspace will lead to increased feelings of satisfaction, productivity, and happiness.

Treat yourself well. If you're the type to skimp on quality things for yourself but would never dare give a sub-quality item to another person, change your thinking. Invest in yourself. Rewarding yourself with premium products and high-quality indulgences is just as important as being generous and helping others. By allowing yourself to partake in what you consider to be a luxury, you realize you're totally worth it (just like L'Oreal has told you for all those years). Holding yourself in the highest esteem is a hugely important step toward any transformational change. Nurturing and caring for yourself are key components in leading the healthiest, leanest, and cleanest lifestyle. Invest in yourself by considering seminars and courses that help you to grow. This can be a yoga retreat, a career seminar, or a personal coaching session. You'll be happy you spent the money on your own development instead of buying 10 killer pairs of heels. (But, hey, one pair isn't a bad idea once in a while.)

Avoid comparing yourself to others. This is a tough one, but it's life-changing when mastered. Focus on what you are good at. Believe it or not, each person excels at many things and skills well beyond what she gives herself credit for. Use your time to focus on your strengths and grow this aspect of your life. By comparing yourself to others, you're spending most of your time wrapped up in what someone else has but you're lacking, instead of focusing on what's going well for you.

BFFs, Frenemies, and More

Friends can be the glue that helps you keep your sh!$ together through breakups, screwups, and the general ups and downs of life. In fact, a UCLA study suggests women's greatest source of strength can be friendships.[48] But friendships can also be a source of extreme stress and confusion for many women. If you find yourself wondering about your friendships and stressing over them, consider examining the types of friends you have. Here is a look at some of the most common friend scenarios and what to do.

Fizzled friendship: This is a friendship that has been long established and made a lot of sense when you were 16, but now you don't find yourself having too much in common or you both have very different outlooks on life. Sometimes these types of friendships are surrounded with guilt because you feel like you should be spending more time together but neither person has much to contribute. If you find yourself in this situation, suggest a meetup with this friend to see if you can reconnect. If it still doesn't seem fun or effortless, the friendship will naturally fizzle, and you can feel good about having tried to salvage it. These friends often become "good acquaintances" vs. close friends, and this type of friend may not know everything in your day-to-day life, and that is okay.

The BFF: Usually this type of friendship stands the test of time, but you can have too much of a good thing. If you get frustrated at your BFF, give yourself space. Are you simply spending too much time with each other? Are you annoyed about something she said or did? Are you taking each other for granted? Even best friends need space. Some of my absolute best friends live on the opposite coast from me and our friendships are still great! Make sure to spend time with other friends to give yourself breathing room. Also remember, best friends are hard to come by; don't take friends for granted or forget to show an appreciation for your friendship.

The frenemy or fake friend: You can't quite figure

out if you're friends, enemies, or a dash of both. Many times these friendships create a lot of stress and anxiety. If you find yourself rolling your eyes at this friend's commentary, or the excuses are getting a little over the top—"Sorry, can't make it because my heater broke (in the middle of summer)"—it is a sign the friendship is over. A frenemy may be saying less than friendly things about you to others or gossiping about your life, which can sting, but unfortunately happens all the time. Frenemies also bring up people and issues from your past that you may be long over, but somehow they want to keep discussing. If this friendship is important to you, consider discussing it with your friend and mention the flakiness, excuses, or gossip. If not, don't stress. You are a good person, worthy of many great friendships, and this happens to not be one of them. Chances are you may be better off without this friend. Use this as a chance to strengthen other friendships and relationships, and recognize that this person is more likely to be a negative influence on your life in the long run.

Remember, not all friendships fulfil all needs. You might need a work friend, a mom friend, a single friend, and a mentor friend. The more, the better!

Mental Health and Mindfulness Summary

- Happiness is a challenging concept. To understand it, you need to understand self-reflection, gratitude, and contentment.
- Being happy is something we all have to continuously work on.
- There are many ways to be happy, but it starts with being grateful for things we have, such as good health, shelter, hot water, and food.
- If you want to be happy, surround yourself with people who are happy or working on this too.
- Engage in work you love. This can be your main job or even a side project. Whatever brings you genuine fun, interest, or motivation can contribute to feelings of satisfaction.
- Mental health and self-care is important to staying on track for a healthy lifestyle.
- Always put yourself first!

The Plan

So you've learned about the right foods, the right workouts, the right state of mind, and now, time to take a nap!

Just kidding! You are going to put all of this info together and let the plan work for you. In just 10 days, you are going to completely transform yourself.

Here's the most effective way to use this program. The best approach is to scan through it to get a sense of what you'll need to do. Then take a look at your calendar and choose the best 10-day block of time. Don't set yourself up for failure by choosing the busiest week of your year! It might be a good idea to start on a weekend, when you probably have a little more time and flexibility. You'll have an action item, each day. Don't worry, some of them will take mere seconds to think about; others might be a longer-range lifestyle change. They'll *all* get you thinking, moving, acting, improving.

10-Day Total Diet Transformation

In this section, you'll find various options for breakfast, lunch, dinner, and snacks that you can choose from for the next 10 days.

Each of the recipes that follow makes one serving. I have provided you a sample meal plan for each day, but if you prefer a different item on the list, you can interchange for whatever other meal options I provided.

Mix it up and try something new each day to avoid getting bored and to keep your metabolism guessing.

And don't forget to drink plenty of fluids. (See "How Much Water Do You Really Need" on page 70 for guidelines on how much you should drink each day.)

On page 207, you'll find a shopping list of ingredients you'll need to make these meals and some of my favorite brands.

PART I

Breakfast

Option 1: Overnight Oats

$1/4$ cup quick cook oats (You can also use steel-cut oats, but the texture is more chewy if you're into that.)

$1/2$ cup unsweetened almond milk

$1/2$ tablespoon chia seeds

1   tablespoon peanut butter or almond butter (I buy the fresh ground at Whole Foods.)

4   almonds

Combine the oats, milk, and seeds in a jar or to-go container and refrigerate overnight. The oats will soak up the milk and expand and soften.

The next morning add the nut butter and almonds.

Enjoy it cold or warm it for 30 seconds for a more cozy meal.

Option 2: 2 Hard-Boiled Eggs (or Eggs Any Style)

2   large, organic eggs

5–7   almonds

Boil the eggs the night before for the easiest out-the-door strategy. To make the best hard-boiled eggs: In a saucepan, cover the eggs with cold water, simmer for 15 minutes, let cool for 20 minutes, and then peel.

If you don't like hard-boiled eggs, any preparation is okay.

Enjoy the eggs with the almonds.

Option 3: Sprouted Grain Bread with Almond or Peanut Butter

1   slice sprouted grain bread or $^1/_2$ sprouted grain English muffin,* toasted

1   tablespoon pure almond, peanut, or sunflower butter (freshly ground or no sugar added)

$^1/_2$ banana, sliced

Spread the bread or muffin with the almond, peanut, or sunflower butter. Top with the banana or eat it on the side.

Note: Sprouted grain bread and English muffins are made by the Food for Life company. They are often found in the refrigerated or frozen section. I like the Food for Life cinnamon raisin muffin.

Option 4: Greek Yogurt Parfait

1   cup low-fat Greek yogurt
(I like Chobani or Fage, but any 2% fat Greek strained yogurt is okay as long as there is no added sugar. Avoid flavored varieties; it should say "plain".)

$^1/_2$ cup chopped strawberries

$^1/_2$ cup blueberries

$^1/_4$ teaspoon goji berries

$^1/_2$ teaspoon coconut flakes and 5-7 chocolate chips, optional

Layer all of the ingredients in a cup or parfait dish.

Place in the fridge for 30 minutes.

You can make it the night before. It's easiest to make 2 or 3 at once.

Option 5: Avocado Roll-Up

2   large, organic eggs
1   tablespoon olive oil or olive oil spray
$^{1}/_{2}$ avocado, peeled, pitted, and smashed
1   whole wheat tortilla (I like the Food for Life brand or
       Trader Joe's whole wheat tortillas because they are
       entirely vegetarian without any animal by-products
       or shortening.)
       Hot sauce (I love Tapatio and Tobasco mixed
       together.)

Scramble the eggs in the olive oil.

Spread the avocado on the tortilla.

Layer the eggs on the avocado.

Top with hot sauce. Roll up and enjoy.

PART II

Bar Breakdown

Most days, I am up at 5:30 or 6 a.m. and have to rush out the door to get my day started. Sometimes I don't have breakfast until I get to my desk and the only thing I had time to grab from the kitchen was a bar. Protein bars or health bars are a *huge* industry that's really taken off in the last 10 years. There are entire aisles dedicated to them in the grocery store, and a new superfood is being utilized to make one every day. While I sometimes grab a bar for breakfast to have with my coffee or tea, not all bars are created equal. Here are some of my favorites that you can swap in for breakfast or snacks if time isn't on your side:

Lärabar Peanut Butter Chocolate Chip

- Calories: 220
- Fiber: 3 grams
- Sugar: 19 grams
- Protein: 6 grams

I like this because it has very few ingredients so you know exactly what you are eating. Sometimes this bar can get a little sweet for me. so I don't recommend having it every day, but a few times per week is a good option.

NuGo Organic Dark Chocolate Almond

- Calories: 190
- Fiber: 3 grams
- Sugar: 13 grams
- Protein: 10 grams

I like this bar because I feel really full after eating and most times it can take me through lunch if needed. I also love it because the chocolate is real dark chocolate, not something fake or modified. I really love the taste and texture.

Rocco DiSpirito's High Protein Chocolate Crunch Bar

- Calories: 200
- Sugar: 0 grams
- Protein: 15 grams
- Fiber: 10 grams

I love this bar because it feels like such a big indulgence or dessert, but it is super healthy and has no sugar and is still high in protein. Additionally, I know the ingredients are very high quality, and each bar is personally handmade.

*If you are interested in purchasing these bars, check out my website at www.shilpimd.com for the link and a promotional code.

PART III

Lunch

Option 1: Spicy Ramen

$1/_4$ onion, chopped

$1/_4$ clove garlic, chopped

2   tablespoons olive oil

3   cups vegetable broth (I like the Pacific or 365 Whole Foods Brand.)

1   cup cooked buckwheat soba noodles or wheat ramen noodles (I like the Annie Chun's brand. Look for it in the international food or pasta aisle.)

2   teaspoons cumin powder

1   teaspoon turmeric powder

$1/_2$ teaspoon chili powder

     Pinch of salt

$1/_2$ cup cilantro

     Salt to taste

Lightly sauté the onion and garlic in a pan with olive oil.

Transfer the sautéed onion and garlic to a larger pot.

Add the vegetable broth. Boil for 2 minutes.

Add the noodles, cumin, turmeric, chili powder, and salt. Boil for 10 minutes.

Top with cilantro and salt to taste.

Option 2: Amy's Quarter Pound "Burger" with Roasted Sweet Potato

$^1/_2$ sweet potato, peeled and diced

2   tablespoons olive oil, divided

1   Amy's quarter pound veggie burger

2   tablespoons salsa (I like Green Mountain or Jack's Gourmet.)

Preheat the oven to 450°F.

In a bowl, combine the diced sweet potato with 1 tablespoon of olive oil. (I just use clean hands to mix it all up!)

Line a baking tray with foil. Place the sweet potatoes on the tray. Bake for 30 minutes, until slightly golden

Meanwhile, cook the burger. Grill the burger in the other tablespoon of oil in a pan. Grill on each side until golden brown. (The burger may remain slightly soft inside but it will be cooked.)

Add salsa on top of burger. Enjoy with sweet potato!

Option 3: Hummus and Veggie Wrap

1	whole wheat tortilla (I like Food for Life or Trader's Joe's whole wheat tortillas.)
1	tablespoon hummus (I like 365 Whole Foods.)
2	teaspoons pine nuts
$1/4$	cup canned olives, rinsed and drained
$1/2$	cup choice of meat, slightly more than half the size of your fist (for example, one small chicken breast, grilled and sliced) or veggies, such as grilled mushrooms or $1/2$ avocado
2	large lettuce leaves

Place the tortilla on a plate. (If it's too cold out of the fridge, you can microwave it for 10 seconds to warm it.)

Spread the hummus on the tortilla.

Top with the pine nuts and olives.

Add the meat and lettuce.

Roll up the wrap, slice it in half for easier pick up.

Option 4: Flatbread Pizza

1   whole wheat flatbread (I like Trader Joe's.)
1   cup pasta sauce of your choice
    (I like Classico Tomato Basil or Cucina Antica.)
1   cup light mozzarella or Swiss cheese (The best
    option is to shred a whole block—no fillers.)
1   cup veggies of your choice
    (I like mushrooms, jalapenos, and red onions.)

Preheat the oven or toaster oven to 375°F.

Place the flatbread on a plate. Pour the sauce on the flatbread. Add the cheese and top with the veggies.

Bake for 10 minutes or until golden.

Option 5: Greek Salad Sandwich

1	teaspoon extra-virgin olive oil
10	olives, chopped, rinsed and drained if canned
$1/4$	red onion, chopped
$3/4$	cup hummus
$1/2$	tomato, chopped
$1/3$	cucumber, chopped
$1/3$	bell pepper, chopped (Any color is okay; I usually pick red or yellow.)
1	cup mixed lettuce
$1/2$	lime, juiced
	Salt, to taste
	Pepper, to taste
2	mini whole wheat pitas

In a medium salad bowl, combine all of the ingredients except the pitas.

Stuff the pitas with the salad mixture.

PART IV

Dinner

Option 1: Zucchini Noodles with Sauce

1	large zucchini	1	cup pasta sauce (I like Classico or Cucina Antica. They have the least amount of sugar.)
1	tablespoon salt		
$1/3$	cup olive oil		
$1/4$	onion, chopped		Basil
$1/4$	clove garlic, chopped		Oregano
	Crushed red pepper		Red pepper flakes
	Paprika, to taste		Black pepper

Use a spiralizer or peeler to create noodles of zucchini. Place the zucchini noodles in a bowl and cover with cold water. Add salt. Soak the zucchini noodles in the salt water for 10 minutes.

Rinse the noodles with cold water and boil for 7 to 8 minutes, or until soft but still crunchy.

Heat the oil in a large skillet over medium-high heat. Sauté the onion and garlic for 1 minute, until the onion is softened but not browned. Sprinkle with crushed red pepper, paprika, and salt to taste. Cook for about 2 minutes, occasionally stirring, until the onion softens. Add the zucchini noodles. Add the pasta sauce. Mix everything well to combine. Simmer on low, until the zucchini is cooked through but still crisp.

Adjust seasoning, and serve hot immediately with red pepper flakes, fresh basil, oregano, and cracked black pepper.

Option 2: Stuffed Peppers

2   peppers (red, yellow, or orange)

$1/_4$ cup onion, chopped

1   clove garlic, minced (You can use garlic powder if
        you don't want to chop garlic.)

$1/_2$ pound ground turkey, beef, or mushrooms

2   tablespoons olive oil

3   kale leaves, stems removed and leaves chopped or
        ripped into small pieces

1   tablespoon pasta sauce

        Taco seasoning (I use Old El Paso Taco Seasoning,
        Original or Hot and Spicy.)

Preheat the oven to 350°F.

Slice around the top of each pepper and pull out the stem.
Remove the seeds and wipe the insides with a paper towel.

Place the peppers in a baking dish. Bake them for 10 minutes to soften.

Meanwhile, sauté the onion, garlic, and meat or mushrooms
in the oil until almost brown. Add the kale. (The kale takes
the least amount of time to cook and will cook in the oven.)

Add the pasta sauce and taco seasoning to the mixture.

Remove the peppers from the oven. Use a spoon to stuff
them with the meat/mushroom mixture.

Bake for 10 minutes, until the tops are golden brown and
the pepper edges look wrinkled.

Option 3: Red Lentil or Chickpea Pasta with Red Sauce

1   cup cooked pasta (Around $^1/_2$ cup uncooked. Red lentil, green lentil, or chickpea pasta is best. I like Tolerant, Banza, or Explore Cuisine brand.)

1   tablespoon olive oil

$^1/_2$ teaspoon dried oregano

$^1/_2$ teaspoon dried basil

1   cup red sauce (Classico or Cucina Antica)

Boil the pasta according to the package directions.

In a separate pan, add the oil, oregano, and basil. Add sauce. Add the pasta to the pan. Stir to combine.

Option 4: Fajitas

1	red bell pepper
1	yellow bell pepper
$^1/_4$	Vidalia onion, chopped
1	cup mushrooms
2	tablespoons olive oil
1	package taco seasoning (I like Old El Paso Taco Seasoning.)
2	cups spinach
2	whole wheat tortillas

In a pan, sauté the peppers, onion, and mushrooms in the oil, until soft.

Add the seasoning and continue to cook.

Add the spinach. Cook for 3 to 4 more minutes until the spinach has wilted.

Place the mixture on the tortillas and roll up.

Option 5: Sweet Potato, Kale, and Mushroom Quinoa

$1/_4$ cup quinoa

1   cup water

$1/_2$ tablespoon olive oil

$1/_2$ small sweet potato, peeled and cut into small pieces

$1/_2$ can button mushrooms

1   chicken breast, optional

$1/_2$ clove garlic

$1/_2$ bunch kale or spinach, stems discarded and leaves torn into small pieces

$1/_4$ cup vegetable broth

$1/_2$ teaspoon salt

$1/_4$ teaspoon black pepper

$1/_4$ cup grated Parmesan cheese (1 ounce)

Place the quinoa and water in a small saucepan and bring to a boil. Reduce the heat and simmer, covered, for 12 to 15 minutes, until the water is absorbed.

Meanwhile, heat the oil in a large pot over medium heat. Add the sweet potatoes and mushrooms and cook, tossing occasionally, for 5 to 6 minutes, until golden and beginning to soften. Stir in the garlic and cook for 1 minute. Add the kale, broth, teaspoon salt, and pepper. Cook, tossing often, for 10 to 12 minutes, until the vegetables are tender.

Serve the vegetables over the quinoa and sprinkle with the cheese.

PART V

Snacks

If you need a snack, it should be because you feel hungry and don't want to go for the office candy bowl. Depending on the foods you are eating, some days you may feel hungrier than others. I recommend one to two snacks a day. Here are some healthy choices:

- 1 large orange or 2 small clementines and 1 wedge Laughing Cow cheese
- 3 cups popped popcorn
- 1 tablespoon hummus and 5 carrots
- 1 tablespoon peanut butter or almond butter and 1 apple
- 1 handful nuts/trail mix
- 8 to 10 tortilla chips and salsa
- ½ Nugo, Lärabar, or Rocco bar (Only half as a snack!)

PART VI

Beverages

- Water
- Sparkling water
- Hot tea
- Iced tea, unsweetened
- Hot water with lemon

ALCOHOL

A recent study from the wine industry nonprofit, Wine Market Council, says millennials drank 42 percent of all wine in the United States in 2015, more than any other age group—an average of three glasses per sitting to be exact. Additionally, overall, women consumed 57 percent of all wine in the United States during the same time period. So basically, a lot of us like drinking, and even more of us like wine. Whatever your drink of choice, alcohol often blurs the big picture (literally and figuratively!).

During the 10-day Total Body Transformation, I recommend avoiding all alcohol. The main reason is because when we drink, our body's ability to sense hunger signals and process food items is impaired. Abstaining will allow you to truly identify your feelings and symptoms related to food, exercise, and mindfulness.

BUT I'M STILL HUNGRY

What now?" Don't panic. The program shouldn't leave you feeling starving, but at the beginning you might feel hungry, but that is okay. Part of the point of the 10-Day Total Body Transformation is to help you recognize your own body's cues again, and this includes hunger signals. If you can't get by on the suggestions above, then you may need to supplement with a little extra so that you're not feeling deprived. The key is to add in foods that will satisfy you and keep you full without loads of unhealthy and processed calories. Here are my favorite things to add to meals to make them more filling:

- 1 egg
- 1 serving of almonds
- 1 small bowl of soup or vegetable broth
- 1 side salad/serving of cooked vegetables

Day 1

Breakfast: 2 eggs any style (See page 179.)

Lunch: Flatbread Pizza (See page 187.)

Dinner: Stuffed Peppers (See page 190.)

Snack: Your choice

Exercise: Walk 20 minutes, or do a HIIT workout.

Water: Your calculated amount (See page 70.)

Mind: Focus on gratitude. Make a list of all the most important relationships in your life (or scroll through all of the contacts on your phone.). Highlight the ones you are grateful for. Select one and write him/her a personal email just to "check in" or see how things are going. Try to select someone you have been meaning to reach out to but haven't had time; it might be a great way to reconnect.

Day 2

Breakfast: Greek Yogurt Parfait (See page 180.)

Lunch: Amy's Quarter Pound "Burger" with Roasted Sweet Potato (See page 185.)

Dinner: Fajitas (See page 192.)

Snack: Your choice

Exercise: Yoga

Water: Your calculated amount (See page 70.)

Mind: Decluttering part one: Pick a space in your life, such as your home office, your closet, or your work desk. Is it perfectly organized, or far from it? Take a moment to sketch out, or find pics online of what you would love the space to look like. Create a space that you are excited to be in by organizing, purging, and cleaning. Being left with only essentials can be liberating and make you more productive.

Not sure where to begin? Follow @NeatMethod on social media for ideas.

Day 3

Breakfast: Sprouted Grain Bread with Almond or Peanut Butter (See page 180.)

Lunch: Hummus and Veggie Wrap (See page 186.)

Dinner: Zuchinni Noodles with Sauce (See page 189.)

Snack: Your choice

Exercise: Try a workout class in your area.

Water: Your calculated amount (See page 70.)

Mind: If you have children, write a letter to your kids about anything you are feeling today. Think about what you would like to say to them when they are older, and then put those thoughts down on paper. You can also email yourself or save it under a draft if that's easier to find.

My husband has a monthly meeting that takes about two hours. During each session, he writes a quick note to our kids before getting on with his other work. It is a great way for him to reflect on them growing up, and it is a built-in time frame.

Is there a time or meeting in your schedule that recurs weekly or monthly? Can you use this to connect with someone important to you?

Day 4

Breakfast: Overnight Oats (See page 179.)

Lunch: Spicy Ramen (See page 184.)

Dinner: Red Lentil or Chickpea Pasta with Red Sauce (See page 191.)

Snack: Your choice

Exercise: HIIT workout (Try Bikini Body Guide or Jillian Michaels.)

Water: Your calculated amount (See page 70.)

Mind: Do something for yourself! Maybe this can coordinate with a weekend, but there is no better time to #treatyoself. My favorite treat yourself activities are mani-pedis and blowouts at the Drybar. Without breaking the bank, pick a splurge and take time to enjoy it! You deserve it.

Day 5

Breakfast: Avocado Roll-Up (See page 181.)

Lunch: Greek Salad Sandwich (See page 188.)

Dinner: Sweet Potato, Kale, and Mushroom Quinoa (See page 193.)

Snack: Your choice

Exercise: Yoga workout

Water: Your calculated amount (See page 70.)

Mind: Find your favorite journal or notebook. If you don't have one, go out and purchase one. This can be a fun activity and is important to have on hand. List your goals for Career, Home, and Life.

Next, think about where you want to be in one year, five years, and 10 years. Now that you have listed the goals, select one and write out an actual action plan. For example, "save money" can be achieved by reading a financial book, meeting with a financial advisor, saving $100 from your salary for retirement, or any other ways that work for you.

Day 6

Breakfast: Sprouted Grain Bread with Almond or Peanut Butter (See page 180.)

Lunch: Hummus and Veggie Wrap (See page 186.)

Dinner: Fajitas (See page 192.)

Snack: Your choice

Exercise: Add 0.5 mph to your last run/walk/jog. Do this for 35 to 40 minutes.

Water: Your calculated amount (See page 70.)

Mind: Set up a lunch or workout date with a friend. Maybe it is a friend who you want to reconnect with or just someone you love to hang out and laugh with.

Day 7

Breakfast: Greek Yogurt Parfait (See page 180.)

Lunch: Amy's Quarter Pound Burger with Roasted Sweet Potato (See page 185.)

Dinner: Zucchini Noodles with Sauce (See page 189.)

Snack: Your choice

Exercise: Do a HIIT workout

Water: Your calculated amount (See page 70.)

Mind: Power down your smartphone. According to statistics: In a recent study of 1,600 managers and professionals, a professor of leadership at the Harvard Business School, found that:

- 70 percent of people said they check their smartphone within an hour of getting up
- 56 percent check their phone within an hour of going to sleep
- 44 percent said they would experience "a great deal of anxiety" if they lost their phone and couldn't replace it for a week.

Pick one day this week when you will shut off your phone during the evening. Choose an activity that you can fill this time with—family time, an outing, sleep, reading a book, or exercising.

Day 8

Breakfast: Overnight Oats (See page 179.)

Lunch: Spicy Ramen (See page 184.)

Dinner: Stuffed Peppers (See page 190.)

Snack: Your choice

Exercise: Try another free class in your area.

Water: Your calculated amount (See page 70.)

Mind: Try some art! Art therapy can be restorative and extremely relaxing. I love coloring with my kids, but there are tons of adult art projects you can do. Find a local pottery place (Color Me Mine is an example) or choose a coloring book or picture and get to work!

Day 9

Breakfast: 2 Hard-Boiled Eggs (See page 179.)

Lunch: Flatbread Pizza (See page 187.)

Dinner: Sweet Potato, Kale, and Mushroom Quinoa (See page 193.)

Snack: Your choice

Exercise: HIIT workout (Try Insanity or workout video/DVD/YouTube.)

Water: Your calculated amount (See page 70.)

Mind: Decluttering part 2: A lot of your personal belongings can make or break your day. If you have tons of things on your desk or in your closet, you can't focus clearly on the objectives and goals you have set out for yourself.

Less is usually more. Find a way to put things away and if you do decide to clean/declutter start by classifying what you have and don't be afraid to get rid of things. If you have piles of unread magazines and books you can either schedule a day to read some of them or get rid of them and end your subscriptions.

Another key to decluttering is deciding not to fill up your space again. This can be the toughest part. But take a few days to bask in your new clean space!

Day 10

Breakfast: Avocado Roll-Up (See page 181.)

Lunch: Greek Salad Sandwich (See page 188.)

Dinner: Red Lentil or Chickpea Pasta with Red Sauce (See page 191.)

Snack: Your choice

Exercise: Yoga workout

Water: Your calculated amount (See page 70.)

Mind: Congratulations! Today is your last day of the Total Body Transformation. Pull out your notebook or journal and jot down what you loved and hated about the 10 days.

Send one note of gratitude to someone who is special to you. This can be an email, a quick text, or a hand-written letter.

Shopping list:

Oats—Mccann's Steel Cut Oatmeal or Quaker Old Fashioned Oats

Almond milk—Unsweetened Almond Breeze or New Barn

Peanut butter—Fresh ground from any store or store bought unsweetened (no sugar added)

Chia seeds-Any brand is ok

Almond butter—Fresh ground from any store or store bought unsweetened (no sugar added)

Almonds

Large organic eggs

Sprouted Grain Muffins—Food 4 Life (Cinnamon Raisin or Plain)

Sprouted grain bread—Food 4 Life (Plain or Low Sodium)

Banana

Lowfat Greek yogurt—Chobani or Fage 2% Plain

Strawberries

Blueberries

Goji berries (optional)—Sometimes these can be expensive but if you buy from the bulk food section this is less expensive and only buy a small scoop

Coconut flakes—Any brand ok, no sugar added

Chocolate chips—60-70% cacao is ideal, I like Ghirardelli brand semi-sweet chips

Olive oil—Bertolli

Avocado

Whole Wheat tortilla—Food 4 Life Brand or Trader Joe's

Nugo Bar—Dark Chocolate Almond is my favorite bar but there are other flavors as well

Lara Bar—My favorite is banana bread and Apple Pie, but any flavor is ok

Rocco's High Protein Chocolate Crunch Bar

Onion

Garlic

Olive Oil

Vegetable broth—365 Whole Foods or The Pacific Brand

Soba noodles or Ramen noodles—Annie Chun's

Cumin Powder

Turmeric Powder

Chili powder

Salt

Cilantro

Amy's Quarter Pounder Burger—Amy's Organic

Sweet Potato

Salsa—Green Mountain or Salsa Jack (Any brand is ok as long as there are no added sugars)

Hummus-365 Whole Foods or Tribe

Pine Nuts

Canned Olives

Chicken Breast, Turkey, Ground Beef

Lettuce

Whole Wheat Flatbread—Trader Joe's Brand

Pasta Sauce—Classico or Cucina Antica (Both have the least amount of sugar compared to other brands)

Mozzarella Cheese Block—This is the *best* way to get unadulterated cheese, buy the block and shred yourself

Mushrooms

Red Onions

Tomato

Cucumber

Bell Pepper—I like any color, I usually go for green, red, and yellow

Lime

Mini Pita Pockets—Trader Joe's Brand

Zucchini

Crushed red pepper

Paprika

Basil

Oregano

Black Pepper

Taco Seasoning—Old El Paso Taco Seasoning packets in original (Spicy is great too but brace yourself)

Kale Leaves

Lentil Pasta—Tolerant, Banza, or Explore Cuisine Brands for lentil pasta

Regular Pasta—Barilla

Quinoa—Lundberg Organic, Near East, or Check the Bulk Foods section

Baby Carrots

Nuts/Trail Mix (Ideally without any candies or candied fruits/nuts)—I buy these nuts in bulk at Costco or BJ's

Tortilla Chips—Green Mountain or SuperEats Sea Salt (High Protein)

Clementine or Orange

Popcorn—Nature's Promise or Any Unbuttered, unsalted popcorn (you can season this yourself with olive oil, coconut oil or salt)

Laughing Cow Cheese-I like the original Swiss flavor

Lifelong
Success

Y ou made it! You're now hopefully feeling high on life and leaner, cleaner, and happier than ever before! Remember, you have the power to design your life and goals and now you also have the tools. Actions are ultimately what shape your future and keep you on the path to success. In order to take action, you should continue to follow the principles, foods, workouts and mental exercises found in the 10-day plan. The more frequently you practice, the more these will become regular habits and fixtures in your life.

You have now figured out what foods you love, what you don't like as much, how to avoid eating mindlessly and a workout that works for you. The goal is to keep yourself on track by continuing to follow the same 10-day principles you have learned. Use these tips to keep on track:

Allow for modifications. If you want to continue following this plan for 10 more days, perfect! But if you do want to reconnect with a friend over a happy hour and are adding back in a small glass of wine, be aware of other changes you may want to make (for example, not skipping exercise that same day, or having a high fiber meal or snack to help metabolize the sugar in wine).

Plan your meals and snacks. A little planning goes a long way. Make sure to have the ingredients at home to make one or two of the meals you liked from the plan. If you do substitute items be careful to read labels.

Eating Out

Eating out is where the struggle gets real.

Don't feel ashamed to make substitutions. Any bread or starch can be substituted with greens.

Ask for sauces on the side instead of saying "light." Everyone's idea of "light" sauce is different.

Avoid a clean plate. Even if you were taught to finish everything on your plate, eat only as much as you need to keep you full. Save the rest and take it home. Even if you eat it in two hours, it's healthier than stuffing yourself with food just because it's in front of you.

Share your healthy habits. Don't be afraid to tell the table you are trying to eat healthy, especially if you feel self-conscious about making changes or substitutions to your order. You are probably not being judged; it's more likely that others are rethinking their own eating habits and orders.

Pick just one. Unless it's your birthday, you're celebrating something big (making it to the weekend after a long workweek doesn't count!), or you're drowning your sorrows (which I don't endorse, by the way), you should avoid having both alcohol and dessert. I like to pick one or the other. Indulging in both is a recipe for disaster.

Tricks for a Boozy Brunch

Hey, I get it. I like a good Sunday brunch and banter sesh with the girls too. But to avoid turning this weekly get-together into a regular excuse to eat like crap, take these tips with you when you're faced with bottomless mimosas.

Choose the meal that has the most protein plus greens. If something comes with greens, make that your first choice. If you get a choice between greens and French fries or another type of potatoes, pick the green salad. Can't bear the thought of a fry-less brunch? Someone at the table almost *always* gets fries, and you can snag a few without eating a whole basket.

Be sure to get fiber with your meals. I keep bringing up the F-word because fiber with every meal will keep you healthy, keep your gut moving, and get you lean and clean.

Make sure this isn't your first meal of the day. So many people make the mistake of heading into a midday brunch on an empty stomach because they think "brunch" indicates a mandatory combo of their first two meals, and anything more would be overly indulgent. Wrong! If you show up at noon ravenous, you're almost guaranteed to inhale anything that looks carby, yummy, and quick. Having a small but balanced mini-meal in the morning means you can show up with steady blood sugar and a craving for socializing, not carbs.

Limit alcohol. Again: bottomless mimosas. I hear you on this one, especially after a night out including margaritas and questionable decisions. But alcohol is the quickest way to kill your inhibitions and throw out all your careful planning and preparation. Avoid the big-girl glass of booze and toast with water instead.

How to Recover from a Bad Eating Day or Weekend

First, don't panic. Don't starve. This situation happens to everyone. If you had a weekend of sports watching and brunching that became an all-day affair, the next day you may feel guilty and gross. You have to forgive yourself and make minor adjustments for next time. Here's how.

Do not skip food the following day. You may be tempted to forgo all your meals the next day to make up for the indulgences, but this creates a large setback in your metabolism. Just don't do it.

Hydrate. Aim to drink at least two liters of water and avoid caffeine.

Drink the right beverages. Ginger ale and club soda with lemon will settle your stomach and help your body return to its natural state.

What to Do about Cravings

Sometimes cravings hit, and all of a sudden mac and cheese is calling your name. Cravings are not always bad as they can signal a flavor, nutrient, or taste your body is missing. Additionally, as your diet changes to more nutrient-rich foods, cravings will start to fade, and if you do feel a craving coming on, you'll know exactly what kind of food to reach for.

Why Do You Get Cravings?

Think about our caveman ancestors for a second. Imagine how they navigated the world. Their bodies helped them make sense of their surroundings, and cravings were meant to signal to them that something was missing. That elusive *something* was a burst of calories they needed to help with survival.

Times may be a little different today, but evolution takes a while to catch up. We still get cravings, but they're not always signs of a life-or-death caloric deficit. Your body does require calories as a form of energy. If you're low on energy, the sluggish feeling triggers a search for a food that is calorically dense to satisfy the craving and, in turn, a part of your brain that is associated with hunger and satiety.

For our ancestors, food was truly used for survival. But fast-forward to now, and it's clear that cravings are usually the result of a poor lifestyle, a diet that lacks vital nutrients, or an imbalance in the cascade of hormones responsible for keeping you full and happy.

Pick your poison: sugar, carbs, or salt. If one or all of these sound like your go-to flavor sensation in times of stress or celebration, you're not alone. These are the most commonly craved foods, and for good reason. Cravings have both a physical and emotional component because they impact **serotonin**, the famous neurotransmitter in the brain that influences your feelings of happiness and correlates with your sensation of hunger. Consuming sugar and carbs increases the release of serotonin, and it can boost your mood temporarily. However, the more you consume, the more you'll require over time to achieve the same effect. This is very similar to how drugs work in your body and in your brain. Depletion of serotonin occurs because of a poor diet, anxiety, and even poor digestion.

Mood and emotional triggers can be another source of cravings. Many times you might associate an elevated mood with a specific food and think that this is the only food that can reproduce that same sense of happiness. These feelings are usually temporary, and if you look closely, these same centers are triggered by healthier activities like exercise and enjoyment. Even just imagining certain food and drinks can cause us to crave them. Research also shows that when subjects are imagining a food item, they have difficulty completing other tasks until they've satisfied the craving.

Other physiological reasons for craving certain

foods are micronutrient and mineral deficiencies. One study found that women who eat low-calcium diets often crave salty foods because sodium can increase calcium levels in the blood for a short period of time after eating. Salt cravings can also be found in women who are slightly deficient in potassium and iron.

Have you ever had a very strong urge to eat chocolate? (Is the sky blue?!) Well, it's not your fault. Chocolate is one of the most powerful triggers of serotonin, and eating it immediately boosts your mood. Beyond that basic need fulfillment, a craving for chocolate can also indicate a magnesium deficiency because cacao is a major source of the micronutrient.

When you crave any sugary food, there's a reason: Sugary foods cause an immediate release of energy into the bloodstream in the form of glucose. This is why when you feel low on energy, you're more likely to reach for something sweet.

Combating Cravings

So now that you know *why* cravings strike, how can you beat them? I have some ideas.

Stay full and satisfied. This means eating when you're *actually* hungry and having a diet that's full of healthy fat and protein. Additionally, if you are not eating the slow carbs we discussed earlier and incorporating foods like whole grains, high-fiber vegetables, and healthy fat into your diet, you'll be more likely to reach for a quick-absorbing carbohydrate like a pastry, candy, or white flour-based product.

Maintain a steady blood sugar. The spikes and dips in blood sugar are what cause your brain to want more of a specific food to achieve a feeling of satisfaction or fullness. This is another reason why eliminating refined foods and foods high in sugar is so important. Artificially sweetened foods are much sweeter than whole foods, making your brain more dependent on receiving unnaturally potent and processed flavors.

Exercise. If you are sensing a common theme here, you're right. Exercise helps with a whole lot of stuff. When you feel a huge craving coming on, it's because your body is searching for a serotonin boost. You can naturally achieve the same rush by engaging in physical activity. The next time you have a sudden craving, take three deep breaths with your eyes closed. Follow this with 25 squats and you may forget all about that craving.

Focus on something else. Concentrate on a non-food-related idea or task that could bring you happiness. This includes window shopping, researching a project or vacation, going outside for a walk or bike ride, or calling a friend.

Add nutrient density. Make sure that you are adding foods to your diet that are high in magnesium, chromium, and zinc. That means including foods like almonds, seeds, avocados, broccoli, eggs, and Brazil nuts. Adding in magnesium can be especially helpful to cut out sugar cravings. Zinc in particular is required for insulin secretion, and a deficiency can cause you to have increased sugar cravings.

Eat fat. An intense sugar craving can sometimes be fought with a healthy fat. This can be a spoonful of coconut oil or guacamole. Fat helps trigger the same centers in the brain without providing that quick sugar rush that's likely to leave you miserable later on.

Keep in mind that cravings are learned. Cravings are often the product of learned behavior. When you frequently get the same cues that are associated with a certain feeling, emotion, or time of day, these cravings can end up starting a cycle that can be broken only by having the food that you're fantasizing about. If every Friday night you eat pizza and brownies, at the end of the workweek, your body will be on the hunt for deep dish and Betty Crocker. Changing these habits can be super challenging because your body learns to release ghrelin during these cravings to make you feel hungry. Not to mention the fact that your insulin levels plummet, exacerbating your starving feelings and leading you straight to Pizza Hut. The best way to combat this vicious cycle? Avoid it entirely. Sidestep the temptation to get into the habit of weekly indulges and reward yourself with healthy activities instead. (A Friday night bath can also be incredibly indulgent, after all.)

Learn the art of replacement. Replacing a food you are craving with a healthy alternative can be just as good. If you're looking for something salty like potato chips, swap it out with a carrot stick or popcorn. Salsa and kale chips are a great way to satisfy that salty desire for nachos and margaritas.

Use leftovers wisely. Sometimes the toughest thing to do can be figuring out what to make or eat. I'm a huge fan of transforming meals from the night before into food for the next day. If I make a salad, I often put the leftovers in a wrap the next day. It's a fresh way to use what's left and still stay on track. If you had chicken with quinoa last night, you can cut the remaining meat into strips and make fajitas for lunch. Listen, I *hate* cooking. I'm not good at it, and I always feel like I could be using my time in better ways. But even I sometimes have to chop stuff and move it around on a skillet to provide for my family.

To be honest, the more I do it, the less eye-rolly I am about it. Kind of.

Binge Eating

We've all had those nights when we can't seem to shut the refrigerator. But whether you realize it or not, **binge eating** can be indicative of a type of eating disorder called **binge eating disorder (BED)**. While it isn't the same as anorexia or bulimia, it can have serious consequences. Many of us can consume more than we mean to if we have been feeling deprived or are eating mindlessly, but people who binge eat may not be able to stop this kind of behavior on their own. If you think you may be suffering with this or any other form of disordered eating, find a doctor you trust and be honest with him or her about all your thoughts and behaviors.

Maybe you don't have BED, but you know you struggle with the occasional binge that leaves you feeling defeated. This isn't your fault. This behavior is often the result of many years of deprivation from wholesome and naturally satiating foods, such as fresh vegetables, organic meats, and pure chocolate, instead of pasta in a microwave container, cookies in a tin, or frozen pepperoni pizzas. Many times, this deprivation

stems from years and years of dieting and a tumultu-
ous relationship with food. If you can change the role
food plays in your life, you can also change how food
affects your life.

We all have triggers for eating, and sometimes
adopting a healthy lifestyle can feel impossible. But
that doesn't mean you're helpless. You can train your
brain to avoid unhealthy choices if you start to
identify your triggers. For me, bottomless snacks or
meals are often the result of boredom or fatigue.
Usually I find myself reaching for sugary snacks when
I haven't slept enough, because I know I can get that
quick energy boost I crave (and will pay for later)
with a surge of sugar.

The Triggers Tripping You Up

Many of us reach for food even when our hunger is
in check. So why do we do it? Here are the most
common triggers. Find out which ones commonly
trip you up:

Boredom: Have you ever had some spare time at
home and found yourself perusing the pantry, then the
fridge, then back over to the pantry? You try some chips,
then some nuts. Then a string cheese, then a handful of
cereal. Back to salty, so you're onto chips again. This is

true bored eating; in other words, you're using food to fill your time. The most important thing to do is recognize this and reroute yourself the next time you're feeling boredom creep in so you're not bored near the kitchen. Use this time to work out, take a warm bath, scroll through Insta, Facebook stalk your ex (no, actually, don't do that), or even nap. You'll probably kill your craving through the sheer power of distraction.

Fatigue: Research shows that the less you sleep, the more likely you are to reach for unhealthy foods.[49] One study even indicates that this can add up to an extra 500+ calories per day.[50] Those extra calories could result in gaining a pound in one week that you could avoid simply by sleeping more.

Emotions: If you've ever felt stressed or down and reached for a brownie or cheeseburger, then you know a thing or two about emotional eating. When we eat based on emotions, we're trying to cope with whatever stress is going on in our lives at the time. (Consider it the food equivalent to too many glasses of wine after marathon meetings.) Because emotional eating is spurred by things like anger, sadness, or frustration, the body craves very specific foods to mitigate these feelings. Pizza, nachos, cookies, ice cream, etc., all are high in fats, salt, and sugar. Have you ever gone through a bad breakup and wanted nothing more than a big, kale-filled salad? Or had a rough day at work and wished you had a stick of celery? Yeah, I didn't think so. It's because your brain is wired to crave the unhealthy foods that will lead to an immediate mood shift. But as you already know, that shift comes with a big price.

Eating Mindfully

If you ate your last meal somewhere on the freeway between work meetings, it's time for a serious crash course in **mindful eating**. This is the practice of paying attention to what you're putting in your mouth and actually listening to and thinking about your hunger cues. Being mindful of the food that you're consuming takes a lot more effort than you think. When you eat mindfully, you're eating with purpose and intention. Mindful eating also means focusing on hunger cues and determining whether or not you *are* hungry, and if so, what type of food you actually want (not just the food that's in front of you or the one that looks so damn good in the TV commercial).

Mastering mindful eating means understanding why you eat food and understanding what foods you often reach for. You already know all the physical reasons you may reach for certain types of food, but many physical and emotional triggers can cause cravings and lead you to eat certain foods too. Becoming aware of these physical and emotional triggers can help you eat more mindfully and consume nutrient-rich foods that will leave you full of energy and excited for life.

Eating mindfully is also a major skill to hone because it can dissuade you from filling your plate out of frustration, boredom, or habit. It allows you to actually enjoy the experience and pleasures associated with consuming good food. (Trust me, there are sooo many.) Being mindful of what you eat requires you to think of *why* you eat, *what* you want to eat, *how much* you want to eat, and whether or not eating satisfies your hunger or fills a different kind of void. Although mindfulness takes practice, you can become a true master by learning to understand what your body needs and why, and providing it with the nourishment and sustenance it requires day after day.

We've all been there: faced with a plate of warm, gooey chocolate chip cookies, and feeling compelled to stuff our faces even if we aren't hungry. Oftentimes, you might feel powerless against food because, as you've learned, it can be a powerful trigger of pleasure centers in your brain. But you *can* take back control and stay on track no matter the circumstances. Here's how.

Enjoy your meal at a table. This is a big one: Eat at a table rather than in front of the TV or at your desk or with your phone glued to your hand. Everyone's a multitasker, but all these distractions lead us to consume foods mindlessly and without pleasure. Sitting down to enjoy a meal is the most ideal way to focus on what you're eating, and taking these few moments as a restorative and meditative break can totally change your day. This practice gives you space to take a time-out from the daily chatter of technology and a busy workday.

Remember: You can have it tomorrow. Many times, we're driven to eat foods that we view as a treat for fear that we won't be able to have them again or that they're a limited time offer. When you see that plate of cookies in front of you, the visual cue alone triggers your brain to quickly scramble to get one because you think, *"what if someone else snags the last one?"* I've totally dealt with that territorial instinct too.

Stop to think for a minute: We're all adults here. If you want to eat a chocolate chip cookie, you can probably have one later. You can bake some, buy some, or order some online. Despite what your brain is telling you in the moment, we are not suffering in the age of a cookie famine. There isn't a shortage of these items, and the satisfaction you achieve from resisting this temptation will begin to take a stronger and more gratifying hold over you than actually consuming the cookie itself. Making a decision to actively *not* eat something just because it's in front of you is a major success that will help you reclaim some power over food instead of letting food control you.

Eat slowly. This can be challenging for everyone, especially me! But eating slowly helps you become more aware of what you're putting in your mouth. By slowing down, you can consume fewer calories and actually taste the food you're eating. What a concept! This slowing down naturally helps you to ingest a reasonable portion size. When you eat food slowly and chew each bite, it allows your taste buds the time to fully experience and enjoy each morsel. Plus, slower eating can keep you from developing gas and bloating. (And from burning the roof of your mouth.)

Don't peak too soon. When you get to a party or event, head to the bar and grab a club soda with lime. Sip slowly and take a lap around the room to see what food options are available. Survey each one carefully to determine if it's really what you want. Are you tempted by desserts because you just have an innate sweet tooth? Or because you really want a dessert? Maybe you're actually feeling something more savory. Sip your bubbly water to put the brakes on your impulses and allow you the time and space to tune in to your cues.

Use high-quality ingredients. To truly get the most of your healthy fare, use high-quality produce, grains, and spices to prepare your meals. You wouldn't put cheap lotion on your face if you knew it would give you a rash, right? Well, cheap or processed ingredients cause inflammation inside your body the same way knockoff drugstore creams cause inflammation all over your T-zone, so always think twice about the ingredients you use and consume. Sometimes high-quality ingredients come with a hefty price tag, so to save yourself from breaking the bank, purchase them in small quantities. Need fresh Parmesan cheese? Buy a small chunk instead of the huge wedge to avoid waste, and you'll enjoy and appreciate it more.

Consider the importance of food in your life so you can make the experience enjoyable. Whether you're short on time or it's just a force of habit, you may be scarfing your food without actually getting any good feelings from it. But every meal or snack can be fun, relaxing, and pleasurable. Having a snack? Put your nuts or veggies in a nice bowl. Use real silverware or a nice lunch plate to accompany your food. Carve out time to just take in the sight, taste, and smell of your food without distraction.

Dear Reader,

Congratulations! You did it! You made a commitment to yourself and hopefully you finished the 10 days without too many bumps in the road. Any time you start a journey to better yourself or learn more about the world around you, challenges are common. But remember, this is how you grow!

I hope that you found the 10-Day Total Body Transformation useful, informative, and fun. You can use the information in this book as a guide and always return to it if you need a refresh or reboot. Making a conscious decision to maintain a healthy mind, body, and soul is not easy, but know that you are stronger and smarter than you realize.

We are on this journey together and I am here to help you. I hope you will share your stories and questions with me and the 10-Day Total Body Transformation community. Follow me on social media @ShilpiMD and use #10DayTBT.

All My Best,
Dr. Shilpi

Endnotes

1   http://www.apa.org/news/press/releases/stress/2012/gender.aspx

2   http://www.medscape.org/viewarticle/502825

3   http://www.ncbi.nlm.nih.gov/pubmed/20604869

4   http://www.pewresearch.org/fact-tank/2016/12/13/whats-on-your-table-how-americas-diet-has-changed-over-the-decades/

5   http://www.health.harvard.edu/blog/eating-too-much-added-sugar-increases-the-risk-of-dying-with-heart-disease-201402067021

6   https://www.accessdata.fda.gov/scripts/InteractiveNutritionFactsLabel/sugars.html

7   http://www.who.int/mediacentre/news/releases/2015/sugar-guideline/en/

8   http://ajcn.nutrition.org/content/86/4/895.full

9   http://www.ncbi.nlm.nih.gov/pubmed/18769702

10   http://advances.nutrition.org/content/4/2/226.abstract

11   http://jama.jamanetwork.com/article.aspx?articleid=1693739

12   https://www.ncbi.nlm.nih.gov/pmc/articles/PMC2699871/

13   https://www.ncbi.nlm.nih.gov/pubmed/12079860

14   http://www.nhlbi.nih.gov/health/educational/wecan/eat-right/distortion.htm

15   http://jama.jamanetwork.com/article.aspx?articleid=195813

16   https://www.niddk.nih.gov/health-information/health-statistics/Pages/overweight-obesity-statistics.aspx

17   http://www.psu.edu/ur/2003/valuemeals.html

18   http://www.jstor.org/stable/10.1086/662615

19   http://foodpsychology.cornell.edu/discoveries/stopping-serving-size

20   http://www.bmj.com/content/349/bmj.g6015

21   http://www.health.harvard.edu/staying-healthy/abdominal-fat-and-what-to-do-about-it

22   http://news.yale.edu/2000/09/22/stress-may-cause-excess-abdominal-fat-otherwise-slender-women-study-conducted-yale-shows

23   http://www.journalsleep.org/ViewAbstract.aspx?pid=27724

24   http://ajcn.nutrition.org/content/87/4/801.full

25   http://journals.plos.org/plosone/article/file?id=10.1371/journal.
        pone.0057873&type=printable

26   http://onlinelibrary.wiley.com/doi/10.1111/jgs.13376/abstract

27   http://ajph.aphapublications.org/doi/abs/10.2105/AJPH.2013.301556
        ?journalCode=ajph

28   https://www.nature.com/nature/journal/vaop/ncurrent/pdf/
        nature13793.pdf

29   http://www.andeal.org/topic.cfm?cat=4089

30   http://www.tandfonline.com/doi/abs/10.1080/10773525.2015.11060
        75?journalCode=yjoh20&

31   https://www.acsm.org/docs/brochures/high-intensity-interval-
        training.pdf

32   https://www.unm.edu/~lkravitz/Article%20folder/HIITvsCardio.
        html

33   https://www.ucsf.edu/news/2010/05/4411/brief-exercise-reduces-
        impact-stress-cell-aging-ucsf-study-shows

34   https://cals.arizona.edu/cpan/best.phtml

35   http://www.health.harvard.edu/healthbeat/exercise-advice-for-
        people-with-heart-problems

36   https://www.sciencedaily.com/releases/2006/05/060529082903.
        htm

37   https://www.ncbi.nlm.nih.gov/pubmed/12683469

38   https://www.sciencedaily.com/releases/2008/03/080310131529.htm

39   https://sleepfoundation.org/sleep-topics/sleep-drive-and-your-body-
        clock

40   http://psycnet.apa.org/journals/psp/52/1/119/

41   https://www.sciencedaily.com/releases/2016/04/160420102523.htm

42   http://www.aasmnet.org/articles.aspx?id=3869

43   http://www.journalsleep.org/Articles/290409.pdf

44   http://www.cochrane.org/CD003048/INFECTN_probiotics-for-
        treating-acute-infectious-diarrhoea

45   http://newsroom.ucla.edu/releases/changing-gut-bacteria-
        through-245617

46   https://www.ncbi.nlm.nih.gov/pmc/articles/PMC4180002/

47   http://www.gallup.com/poll/175286/hour-workweek-actually-
        longer-seven-hours.aspx

48   http://www.anapsid.org/cnd/gender/tendfend.html

49   https://www.ncbi.nlm.nih.gov/pubmed/27855750

50   http://www.webmd.com/sleep-disorders/news/20120314/
        sleep-less-eat-more#1

About the Author

Shilpi Agarwal, M.D., is a board-certified family medicine physician. She received her medical degree from the George Washington University School of Medicine and completed her training in Family Medicine in Los Angeles. She has a special interest in preventive medicine, women's health, weight management, and healthy living solutions. She has worked to serve several different patient populations, including the uninsured and underserved.

Dr. Shilpi also has a special interest in medical media and is the Good Day DC and Fox 5 DC Chief Medical Contributor. She has also discussed a variety of health and wellness topics on network and cable shows such as CBS On The Couch, Good Day LA, KTLA, and Yahoo TV.

She is regularly quoted in publications such as the *Washington Post*, *Glamour*, *Prevention* Magazine, *Health* Magazine, *Reader's Digest*, *Cosmopolitan*, and Dr. Oz's *The Good Life*, to address current health topics and wellness trends.

Dr. Shilpi has been nationally recognized as the "Go-to Girlfriend Doctor." She works to make medicine and healthy living understandable and attainable for everyone. She can always be found testing and scrutinizing the latest health and medical research and fitness and food trends.

She lives in the Washington DC area with her husband and two boys.

Acknowledgments

There are several people I would like to thank and that have played a critical role in the development of this book. This has been one of my greatest challenges and most gratifying experiences.

To the entire Momosa team, Jennifer Reich, Joanna Williams, Amy Kovalski, Jennifer Schriffert, and Nanette Bendyna-Schuman, I appreciate your dedication and diligence in working with me on this project. Jennifer, you made this process seamless and I very much appreciate your support, hard work, and positive attitude all along the way. I have learned so much and truly enjoyed the experience.

Michelle Konstantinovsky, thank you for all of your help, especially in the early stages when this book was just a lot of thoughts on paper. I am grateful for you.

To my Fox 5 family, I appreciate each and every one of you and thank you so much for your consistent support and encouragement. You are all a pleasure to work with.

Amanda Molina, you have been the best girlfriend and voice of reason during this process and always. You are a brilliant, kind, generous, hilarious and beautiful soul on the inside and out!

Thank you to all my girlfriends. I am forever thankful to a few of you in particular who reviewed the manuscript and provided invaluable feedback for all parts of this book.

I am eternally grateful to my family, especially all four of my beloved parents, my older brothers and sisters, and all of our adorable nieces and nephews. I appreciate your continued support and love.

I also want to express my warmest gratitude to all my patients. Over the years I may have helped you, but in reality you have helped me. I have learned from you and grown because of you. I hope to continue connecting with you and supporting you on your individual health journeys.

Thank you so much to my husband. You are my best friend and my forever love. You are the one to encourage me, handle my craziness, and fill my life with laughter. Thank you for your unwavering support in helping me pursue my passions.

Finally, I want to thank my children. You both are the brightest lights and joys of our lives! My wish for you is to always try to see the good in others, never give up on your dreams, and fill your life with laughter! In the words of your late grandfather, "It is ok to laugh without any purpose. If we don't laugh, life is no good."

Index